SURFER MAGAZINE 50 YEARS

SURFER
MAGAZINE
50 YEARS

EDITED BY SAM GEORGE
FOREWORD BY SHAUN TOMSON

CHRONICLE BOOKS

SAN FRANCISCO

TABLE OF CONTENTS

preceding spread: **ERIC GIESELMAN** AT ROCKY POINT.
opposite: PERFECT FORMS: **KELLY SLATER**, TAHITI.

FOREWORD

BY SHAUN TOMSON

SHAUN TOMSON HOLDS OPEN THE FIRST MONTHLY ISSUE OF *SURFER* WITH '76 WORLD CHAMPION PETER TOWNEND (FAR LEFT) AND CINEMATOGRAPHER DICK HOOLE (FAR RIGHT). BURLEIGH HEADS, AUSTRALIA, 1977.

A MAGAZINE'S LIFE IS RELATIVELY BRIEF from publication to pulp. It comes in the mail or is bought at a counter, and is opened and read, usually just once. It might remain around the house for a week or two. It may be opened again, but its journey to the dumpster is assured. There is only one exception to this rule of assured destruction.

Just out of sight and just beyond reach, in attics and basements, in boxes and cupboards, all across the world, are stacks of tattered old SURFER magazines that have been with their owners through adolescence into adulthood, from working life into marriage and parenthood. Almost all of them have been seriously read—I mean really bored into—not just skimmed

through once or twice like the hundreds of other titles available on the newsstand that are then set aside for the trip to the trash. These magazines have been studied as intently as the Talmud is studied by a yeshiva student, and most probably with even more fervor. These journals mark moments in the life of each owner. Every issue represents not only a collection of pictures and articles but also a freeze-frame of its owner's youth. SURFER is not just a magazine but is the framework for a surfing existence, a collection of reference points for an obsession— thinking about that next swell coming down the horizon, planning the new custom board, or pondering that next trip to an outpost on the other side of the world.

I am involved with many different public events around the country—book signings, talks, charity projects, and movie openings. Often someone will hand me a SURFER for an autograph, and the mag is always more than thirty years old. "I bought this issue when I started surfing"; "I got this in my last year in high school"; "I read this while I was on the North Shore"; "This was my favorite cover." Each story and circumstance is different, but there is a common thread running through all of them: One particular SURFER magazine represents a special moment in the owner's life, and for that reason it was impossible to throw away. SURFER represents youth, freedom, and a time when absolutely nothing was more important than that next wave coming down the line. SURFER is a deeply personal photo album, and even though the photos may be of someone else, each different issue represents a snapshot of a surfer's life at that time. Just as we don't throw away photo albums, we don't throw away SURFER.

SURFER magazine was with me when I started out on my surfing journey, 10,000 miles away from California in Durban, South Africa. I can remember that first wave on a board like it was yesterday. It was 1965 at the Bay of Plenty, and I was nine years old. Our beach was a narrow stretch of sand wedged between a ribbon of Miami-style hotels and apartments on the west and the Indian Ocean on the east. The beach had always been a big part of our family life; my earliest memories are of sitting on the sand with my mom and dad beside me, with a big hamper of food in front of us and an umbrella overhead.

That first wave at the Bay: I waxed up with a candle and made my way out through the *shorie*, the impact zone where the waves broke right on the sand. With the world to my back and the horizon ahead, I was truly on my own. The foam rumbled toward me. I swung my board around, dug my little arms hard into the water, and paddled. The whitewater picked me up, shot me forward, and I leaped to my feet and stood up. That feeling of stoke instantly imprinted itself on my being; happiness and fear, exhilaration, speed, and conquest all melded together into one rush of sensation. And the view—that overview of land, looking over and above it all, racing along on an invisible band of energy three inches above the water, separated by just a little sliver of glass fiber. And for a brief moment, I was a master of my little universe. Surfing right there right then gripped me hard and fast and just never let go.

I was in my own compressed surf world of school, home, and the Bay of Plenty, all within a 5-mile radius. Then my dad bought me my first

SURFER. As I sat there in a comfy chair in the living room, bare feet on an old dark wood floor, and sank down into the soft folds of the upholstery slowly turning the pages, I was whisked away to a new world I knew absolutely nothing about. I had been living in a parallel universe, and SURFER was the bridge to the other world. The surf explosion of the '60s just never penetrated South African mainstream culture the way it did in the United States. Surfing was confined to the beach and to surfers, and it never moved off the sand into the national psyche. The California beach-party lifestyle was totally unknown to us kids in culture-controlled, apartheid South Africa. We were insulated from American pop culture. South Africa had no TV, no *Gidget*, no *Lucy*, no *Gilligan*, no *Wide World of Sports*. Since we were a former English colony with strong social and economic ties to the mother country, a lot of what we saw, read, and listened to came from England. Rugby, cricket, and tennis were the big sports, and on state-controlled AM radio, the Beatles, not the Beach Boys, were dominating the charts. But when I read that first SURFER, my world changed completely, and a whole new horizon opened up. Huge waves at Sunset Beach and Waimea Bay in Hawaii, Mickey Dora trashing his trophies and mooning the crowd at Malibu, competitors at the U.S. Championships with Toptex helmets charging the pier at Huntington Beach. Innovative surfboards and amazing models by Hansen, Weber, Bing, and Hobie; The Trestles Special, The Performer, and The Ugly. And coolest of the cool surfing apparel and shoe brands like Hang Ten, Jantzen, Keds, and Pendleton. I found out about David and Dewey and the Duke and knew that if I ever bought a pair of baggies, I had to wear them low on my hips, and they just had to have *the* logo of two little embroidered feet.

That first magazine began a lifelong fascination with SURFER. I knew there was going to be something new and radical in every issue, and I'd always just blast through looking for that one maneuver that would stop me with a WOW. SURFER was a window into the heart of surfing. It told me where the change was happening, and if I read between the lines, really drilled into it, I heard the heartbeat of surfing and knew where we were going: who was hot, what was hot, and what the latest discoveries were. David Nuuhiwa became my favorite, and then later I saw him in films—statuesque, with that royal nonchalant style, unhurried and elegant.

I would read and reread the magazine, the copy becoming imprinted on my brain. I would remember every caption to every photo. I would pore over every ad and then go through and read it all again. Each copy was treasured and

kept in a growing stack. As the copies became worn out, I'd carefully tape the pages together. It wasn't that the magazines aged and started to deteriorate. I'd just wear them out through overreading. Back then the magazine came out only every two months, and in South Africa it was the only surfing magazine available, so there was a lot of wear and tear between issues. Years later, I'd pick up an issue and remember exactly where I had been when I first picked it up.

I can still remember being mystified by a line of copy from that first SURFER I read forty-five years ago. It was a quarter-page black-and-white picture, about center page. The surfer was midway through an ungainly wipeout, only one foot on the board. The caption read, *Even Phil has 'em.* "What does this mean?" I thought. "Who is Phil and what does he have that is so unique it deserves mention?" It took me a few issues to work out that Phil Edwards was one of the world's best surfers and that even the Great One occasionally had a wipeout.

My favorite of all time: I was seventeen years old, at boot camp in the South African Army, four weeks into it and 400 miles from home in the apartheid capital of Pretoria. I'd been screamed at and shot at, gotten little sleep, and generally been drilled on the parade ground into numb submission. We lined up in our squads to receive our mail, and the corporal handed me a SURFER my dad had sent me. A perfect, ultra-miniature left broke on a beach somewhere, and that magazine immediately took me away from where I was to exactly where I needed to be. And that is what the magazine has always done for millions of us all around the world.

I still get my SURFER every month. Now it comes in the mail, and I don't have to go down to the corner shop. Sometimes, though, when I'm wandering through an airport in Los Angeles, Salt Lake, or Phoenix and there is a new SURFER on the stand that has made it there before my mailbox, I can't just walk by and go on my way. I'm absolutely compelled to open it, and I'm instantly transported back in time, into that little surf-stoked boy in the corner café in Durban, absorbing all the newness, looking out at a distant world of perfect waves, and dreaming of going someplace else, to where I needed to be.

INTRODUCTION

BY SAM GEORGE

THERE'S THE WEATHER, AND THEN THERE'S SURFER. During the past fifty years, no two elements have affected the surfer's life more profoundly.

Surfers, after all, are completely dependent upon the weather. Their whole glorious trip hinges on a complicated series of meteorological quirks. True riders on the storm, they base an entire lifestyle on the flapping of a butterfly's wings in some distant hemisphere and the resulting phenomena of spinning low-pressure systems and wandering jet streams. And for the surfer, this atmospheric system is more fragile than it seems. In many cases, the entire course of surfing history has turned on a single day upon which the Weather Gods have smiled. Banzai Pipeline, December 15, 1962: 8- to 10-foot west swell, light northeast trades, blue skies, front lighting, and a cluster of cinematographers on the beach and Butch van Artsdalen in the water. A north swell and kona winds on this day could have set modern tuberiding back an entire season, with incalculable aftereffects. For that matter, what might not have resulted had Bruce Brown and crew rocked up to South Africa's Cape St. Francis on a typical day rather than for the freaky four hours of fantasy they captured on film? We all might still be searching

for an endless summer rather than the "perfect" wave. Surfing's time line is spiked with examples like these, where vagaries of weather have been directly responsible for major perception shifts in virtually every aspect of exploration and discovery, performance, surfboard design, personality, and photography: The clean, back-lit day in 1967 when Bob McTavish and Nat Young rode their V-bottoms in perfect Honolua Bay; the fabulous swell that Larry Yates and team caught at Tamarin Bay while filming *The Forgotten Island of Santosha*; the two weeks of perfection at Pipeline and Off-the-Wall in 1976–77 that gave birth to the Free Ride Generation. And then more modern zeniths: El Nino's '83 Rincon masterwork starring Al Merrick and Tom Curren; the "Jay Moriarity Crucifix" morning at Mavericks in January of '95; Curren again, riding that big day at Bawa on the tiny Fireball Fish; and Laird Hamilton's "oh my god" tube at Teahupoo. In each case, a complex amalgamation of natural forces aligned for the briefest interlude yet created a paradigm-bending moment of collective consciousness for surfers the world over.

SURFER has been there for every one of those moments. Or rather, each of those moments has been presented for the surfer's consideration in the pages of SURFER. Not merely the

groundbreaking highlights—every one of the aforementioned debuted in the magazine—but all those less obvious cosmic coincidences that have, in the five decades since SURFER began publication, helped shape the framework of this thing we call the surfing life: where we surf, how we surf, what we ride, what we look like, and how we perceive the world of waves.

Consider the very first issue, that now-legendary, thirty-six-page black-and-white movie program initially designed to accompany John Severson's 16 mm film *Surf Fever*. Featuring images now referred to as "frame grabs," *The Surfer* was illustrated solely with frozen moments from the film. One depicted a young Mickey Muñoz riding at Arroyo Sequit, head down, arms extended, posed on the nose in his famous hunched-over "Quasimodo" stance. A moment's frivolity, according to Mickey, who asserts he was simply goofing around in the shorebreak. But presented in that seminal issue of *The Surfer*, Mickey's moment was elevated from antic to iconic; soon after the first precious copies of Severson's *The Surfer* made their way to Australia's antipodal shores, surfers up and down the beaches of Sydney could be seen "cracking the curl" with their heads dutifully tucked between their legs, feeling, no doubt, totally relevant.

PAGE 8

Today, a half century later, among the remote islands of Western Sumatra, isolated villagers who a single generation ago had seen few white men, let alone surfers, now describe the fabulous waves that peel along the archipelago's fringing reefs on particularly good days as being "like magazine."

In the mid-'60s, SURFER told surfers to noseride: They rode the nose. In the early '70s, SURFER told us the North Shore was where it was at: Surfers from Cayucos, California, to Middletown, Rhode Island, vainly waxed up seven-six Pipeline pintails. Over the decades they told us to wear matching windbreakers, itchy Mexican pullover sweaters, Day-Glo trunks with 2-inch inseams, superbaggy board shorts with 21-inch inseams, and clunky skateboard shoes to the beach—and we did.

Okay, so they didn't always get it right. SURFER was at least six crucial months behind the curve when it came to the design tumult known as "The Shortboard Revolution." The story of the industry's leading surfboard manufacturers storming into John Severson's Capo Beach office to demand he deliberately sit on the shortboard story at least through the summer of 1967—long enough for them to move their existing inventory of nine-sixes—is one of surfing's great apocryphal tales. But true or not, it handily attests to the influence SURFER wielded.

Yet as much as SURFER has turned its gaze outward to the wider world of waves, it remains the most personal of publications, inexorably bent to the creative will of an eclectic parade of editors and contributing writers.

In the beginning, there was John Severson, the magazine's founder and perhaps the most broadly accomplished creative force in surfing history—artist, filmmaker, photographer, writer, publisher, and all-around waterman, in both big waves and small. Today's equivalent would be a performer like Shane Dorian filming *Momentum*, producing the poster art, shooting the accompanying photos, writing the feature, and then creating and publishing a magazine in which to run it all.

Although Severson's *The Surfer* was crafted with serious artistic intent, the early issues took on an oddly straight-laced editorial stance, as if the magazine was not quite sure of its footing, not confident enough to declare just how far this new beach-bound culture had already split from the Brylcreemed world of mainstream sport.

"Each spring, summer, fall, and winter edition will bring you the tops in surf photography and accurate surf coverage," an editorial succinctly claimed in the very first quarterly issue in 1961. "John Severson will photograph and illustrate THE SURFER and will bring you informative articles on the surfing world."

Strange, then, that this seminal "just the facts, ma'am" mission statement appeared in an issue that featured on its cover a cartoon: Murphy, conceived and drawn by fledgling soon-to-be staff artist (and counterculture icon) Rick Griffin. Murphy was the embodiment of the feckless gremmie, surf-knotted, bleached blond, and browned by many days of skipped school, trunks slung insouciantly low; every Rotarian's nightmare.

The Surfer almost immediately evolved past the "informative articles on the surfing world" stage into a much more dynamic creature. The travel stories, contest coverage, and latest photography were served up with regular portions of art, fiction, and even poetry (though the poetry was, for the most part, pretty awful). The incredible aesthetic diversity that characterized the early SURFER merely reflected its creator.

Each successive editor added his voice to the arrangement. Patrick McNulty (1965–68) was the most unlikely helmsman. A legitimate journalist, McNulty was a domestic and foreign correspondent for the Associated Press before taking the reins from Severson mid-decade. What a guy who'd interviewed John F. Kennedy, Charles de Gaulle, and Nikita Khrushchev found interesting about J. J. Moon and Mickey Dora is, at first, hard to fathom. Then again, there was something affirming in the idea that the 1965 World Championship in Peru or the North Shore winter season of 1967 deserved as much journalistic integrity and commitment as did, say, the Algerian war for independence or a coup d'état in the Congo (both covered by McNulty during his AP days).

Drew Kampion was McNulty's polar opposite—the latter's strident editorials railing against long hair and pot smoking were aimed straight at the new generation of surfers like Kampion. This cultural evolution is the most likely reason Severson decided, during 1967's Summer of Love, to hand over the keys to a young, relatively untested editor. From 1968 to 1971, Kampion turned SURFER into his own bimonthly bohemian rhapsody. SURFER was its boldest, bravest, and most bizarre on Kampion's watch, his obsession with Bob Dylan (who, to the best of our knowledge, doesn't surf) notwithstanding.

The subsequent editor, Steve Pezman, certainly surfed. He was a card-carrying member of the Long Beach Surf Club, early North Shore acolyte, surfboard shaper, and Mexican surf trail sojourner. After writing a couple of design

THE SURFER

SURFER ISSUE NUMBER ONE: PERHAPS THE MOST CULTURALLY INFLUENTIAL MOVIE PROGRAM EVER PRINTED.

and travel stories for *Peterson's Surfing* magazine, Pezman was hired then, almost as suddenly, placed in charge of the whole SURFER machine—Severson having made his statement and moved on to Maui. Once he recovered from the shock of abandonment, however, Pezman took SURFER forward into its most cohesive incarnation, setting a tone that reflected like polished steel the soulful mood of the sport. One particular run of fifteen classic, groundbreaking issues—January 1975 to May 1977—will probably never be equaled.

A pair of wanderers followed. The late '70s found Jim Kempton sitting in the editor's office, once described by Steve Pezman as "a bluff overlooking the whole surfing world." Kempton was all about insight; having lived for a spell in a van with Mickey Dora along the south coast of France, how could he be anything but? Kempton's stay in the venerable Camino Capistrano offices was simply one stop on a grander surf tour, each issue a new dispatch. But there was also an underlying confidence: Kempton approached SURFER as if he were writing liner notes to a great new album he'd discovered six months before anyone else.

Paul Holmes, to whom Kempton passed the baton in 1982, was already an accomplished magazine editor, having previously run *Tracks*, Australia's most subversive surf tabloid. Yet as a former surfboard shaper and pro surf promoter, Holmes brought quiet authority to a SURFER that might have been reduced to a mere observer in the earliest days of the Great Surf Boom. Holmes benefited greatly from his second-in-command, a former Katin Contest semifinalist named Matt Warshaw. Warshaw put enough of his fiercely intelligent stamp on the magazine that it's easy to forget his tenure as editor after Holmes lasted only one year. Deconstructing myths was Matt's forte—questioning their validity in the face of what he saw as a rational passion. He left a big impression: The period in which he edited the magazine, though actually very brief, is often referred to by SURFER aficionados as "The Warshaw Era."

Steve Hawk's tenure was anything but brief—the lanky, spectacled regular foot spent more time at the top of the masthead than any other editor. Beginning in 1991, Hawk presided over an extraordinary period in surf culture, a nine-year roller-coaster ride in which the magazine had to process everything from modern longboards to Merrick "Glass Slippers," from Mavericks to the Mentawais, from Christian Fletcher aerials to Lairdman tow-ins; from the rise of Kelly Slater to the death of Mark Foo. Hawk put Lisa Andersen on the cover and sent Dave Parmenter to Alaska, all the while conducting (and cosseting) perhaps

the greatest collection of surf journalists ever assembled, including Parmenter, Daniel Duane, Bruce Jenkins, Matt Warshaw, Matt George, and Steve Barilotti. Hawk also mentored the young Evan Slater, who sat in the driver's seat for a few laps in the waning months of the millennium before moving on to establish his own voice at a rival surf magazine.

In Slater's mold, however—that of the hot, formerly sponsored pro surfer turned magazine editor—came Chris Mauro. In examining Mauro's editorial contribution to SURFER, only a single anecdote is needed. While on assignment in Indonesia covering a surfing version of the Monterey Pop Festival—an exclusive Sumatran boat trip that included Kelly Slater, Shane Dorian, Rob Machado, Ross Williams, Brad Gerlach, Luke Egan, and Jack Johnson—Chris incurred the ire of an accompanying film crew. "Catching too many good waves," they said. With that sort of credibility, Mauro endeavored to make every reader feel like a "first person."

And me? Having begun writing for SURFER in 1991—and having sat in the editor's chair for the first few eventful years of the new millennium—I've added my own voice to SURFER's story. Of course my relationship with the magazine goes back much further than that; I've been looking at SURFER as long as I've been watching the weather. (In fact, I didn't begin to watch the weather until I began reading SURFER.)

But in assembling this volume, an encapsulation of SURFER's fifty-year history, we decided to establish a template much less, let's say, mercurial than the jet stream. Chaptered as separate spheres of influence—surf discovery, surfboard design, performance, personality, culture, and photography—the entire scope of the magazine can be examined and appreciated for a much more basic contribution to our lifestyle: fifty years of stoke.

This book, then, is dedicated to the talented people who have had a hand in banking those coals: the editors, writers, art directors, and photographers who for more than half a century have provided just about everything a surfer needs but waves.

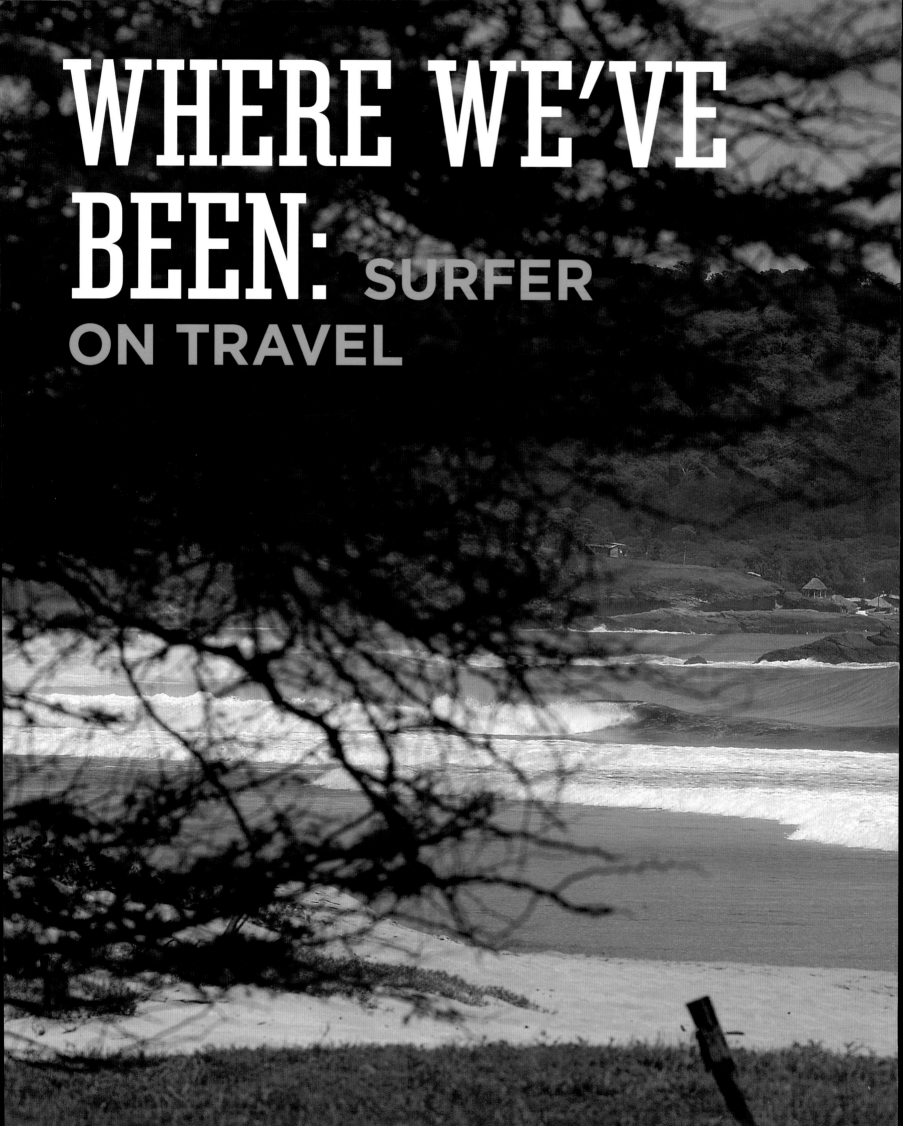

WHERE WE'VE BEEN: SURFER ON TRAVEL

WANDERLUST

"IN THIS CROWDED WORLD THE SURFER CAN STILL SEEK AND FIND THE PERFECT DAY, THE PERFECT WAVE, AND BE ALONE WITH THE SURF AND HIS THOUGHTS."

When he penned this classic manifesto in the very first issue of *The Surfer*, could founder John Severson have imagined where it would lead? This was 1960, remember, when the shape of the surfing world was, if not completely flat, not spherical either. The seeds of recreational wave riding had by that time blown on the trade winds from Waikiki to distant shores, growing into small pockets of stoke in places like the U.S. mainland, Australia, New Zealand, Peru, and France. And yet for surfers in those regions, maps still had plenty of blank spots, the globe itself marked with lines of unfamiliar latitudes and longitudes. In 1960, a run up the California coast to Santa Cruz was still an adventure; Sydney surfers had only just begun to push out from their urban beaches, as yet unaware of the vast watery riches that lay to the north, south, and west. Then came *The Surfer*. In that first issue, thirty-six pages of fractured fonts, "Quasi-modos," the "Malibu Lizard" short story, and a portrait of the hand-painted "Sunset Special"

North Shore tour car, came a spare, twenty-six-word coda steeped in an angst yet unmanifested in that period's innocent lineups.

> In this crowded world, the surfer can still seek and find the perfect day, the perfect wave, and be alone with the surf and his thoughts.

And just like that, Malibu was no longer enough.

Funny, but SURFER magazine didn't seem to know this at first. There was plenty of distant surf in those first issues: Australia, Peru, Hawaii . . . Northern California. But in its first few years of publication, SURFER's presentation of exotic waves was definitely in the "look what's going on over there" vein; the urge to be "over there" yourself was just coming to life. That particular element was introduced with the very first travel cover in 1966. Along with the headline "The Fabulous French Surf" and Aussie John "Wheels"

In this crowded world the surfer can still seek and find the perfect day, the perfect wave, and be alone with the surf and his thoughts . . .

. . . john severson

HOW DIFFERENT THE PERCEPTION OF SURFING MAY HAVE BEEN HAD *SURFER* FOUNDER **JOHN SEVERSON** BASED HIS
SEMINAL MANIFESTO AROUND A CROWDED DAY AT MALIBU RATHER THAN A SOLO SESSION AT HAMMOND'S REEF.

preceding spread: ALL THE ELEMENTS OF SURFARI IN PLACE: THE TREK, THE SOLITUDE, AND WAVES UNLIKE ANYTHING
YOU'VE SEEN AT HOME.

Williams tucked in a hot curl, that cover featured a rather provocative shot of a fetching French surfer kneeling next to her board, her ample bosom spilling out of a tiny Biarritz bikini. Outraged school librarians and uptight moms flooded the magazine with letters of protest, denouncing the eroticizing of what they hoped was developing into a clean-cut sport. Surfers, on the other hand, barely noticed the buxom mademoiselle—they were looking at the fabulous surf and black-and-white and color images that, even alongside the fairly typical travel-guide copy, triggered a collective realization that existing surf maps might be outdated.

Confirmation came quickly. Two issues later the magazine's first real travel story appeared: peripatetic Aussie photographer Ron Perrott's travels through South Africa. More than mere travelogue, this was an actual first-person account of life on surfari. The scenic setups, the surf action (including water shots), new breaks (Seal Point, Jeffreys Bay), the "car with boards on roof in a foreign setting" shot, and local color—all the elements we've come to know so well.

Perrott's groundbreaking feature was followed two issues later by another first: SURFER staff photographer Ron Stoner's trip to mainland Mexico. Stoner's Mexican log had all the elements Perrott had established (Mercury Comet with boards on roof driving through Mexican village? Check.), but added the final touches to the "modern" travel formula that remains in use today, almost a half century later: hot, well-known surf stars (Bob Lenardo, Bill Fury) riding a newly revealed break (Mazatlán) that had been given a pseudonym (Stoner's Point) for the purpose of the feature.

Look at any travel story in a current surf magazine—SURFER included—and see if it doesn't incorporate the template of Stoner's seminal Mexican adventure. And yet while Perrott and Stoner's offerings set a few hardy surf explorers on the trail, traveling to surf was not a widespread movement. In the late 1960s, Hawaii, once an exotic travel destination itself, was presented as the ultimate proving ground, both physically and metaphysically. Meanwhile the late '60s Shortboard Revolution, with its battle cry of total involvement and miniguns, encouraged a more personal relationship with the wave, with the sport's spirit of exploration turning inward toward the mystic eye as well as the tube. Yet while on the surface this new aesthetic may have looked—and smelled—like a Woodstock on waves, there was nothing free about this love. With all this perceived intimacy came a fierce possessiveness and growing sense of entitlement, as if no other surfer deserved the waves quite as much.

"...AND BE ALONE WITH THE SURF AND HIS THOUGHTS."

By 1973, the surfing world had evolved from the Age of Aquarius into the Age of "Locals Only!" The only problem was, there was no place to go that wasn't already crowded with its own pack of surly self-described locals bad-vibing the increasing hordes of unaffiliated surfers wandering from break to break. Small wonder that the surfing world's imagination began to wander too, in alignment with John Severson's first call to action.

> . . . and be alone with the surf and his thoughts.

Emphasis on *alone*. Suddenly it wasn't enough to get the best wave of the day—surfers now wanted every wave. And that sure wasn't going to happen at Rincon. Or Jacksonville Pier, for that matter. How appropriate, then, that in 1973 the first installment of Kevin Naughton and Craig Peterson's epic three-part Central America travel series opened with a simple shot of an unpaved road, leading away from . . . wherever the reader was standing.

Thus began the Golden Era of Surf Travel—and SURFER travel stories. Naughton and Peterson's era culminated in the classic "Discovery on the Way Home from Central America" piece in January '74, which featured the fabulous waves of Petacalco, Mexico. (That the location was not identified did little to mollify a cadre of angry seasonal expats who had laid claim to the hollow beach-break some years before the pair's arrival.) There followed the "Forgotten Island of Santosha" cover story, in which filmmaker Larry Yates and his globetrotting band bewitched the SURFER editors themselves. When he was later asked how he discovered the amazing tropical left-reef break of Santosha, Yates replied that he had read about it in SURFER magazine: an article about the island of Mauritius, which had run in September 1966.

The philosophy of enlightened but ultimately selfish surf searching became the rule: SURFER features no longer presented "what's going on out there," but rather "look what we found . . . and you didn't."

In 1974 it was Bali, albeit described as floating in the South Pacific. Grajagen was next. Then, more mainland Mexico, West Africa, and Baja. A full five years later, fantastic Nias hit the stands, the magazine having been distracted by the Free Ride Era. The first all-travel issue appeared in 1980, featuring, very appropriately, a Craig Peterson shot looking out of a tent at a ripping Abreojos tube. SURFER's first twenty years had shrunk the globe considerably. The next thirty compressed it down to the size of a marble—a blue marble, with waves being discovered and ridden everywhere. Fiji, Tahiti, Java, western Australia, the Caribbean, New Zealand, South Africa: Throw your dart at the map and you'll hit a spot SURFER introduced to its fantasy-travel-hungry readers. SURFER presented a veritable kaleidoscope of empty lineups and perfect tubes—the feature articles that stuffed a thousand board bags.

Some of these stories stand out, however, for the lasting impact they've had on the surfer's perception. Consider the debut of the Mentawai Islands in Sumatra and the Rip Curl promo trip that introduced the wider world to the mind-bending uniformity of "Macaronis." Tom Curren's presence as one of the crew members on this proto–boat trip guaranteed action, but the trip's impact was even greater: The ensuing surf-charter industry made a floating boomtown out of sleepy Padang, shuttling surfers into contact with the isolated Mentawai people, many of whom had never seen a white man until the ones with baggy trunks and boat-deck Mohawks came cruising up over the horizon.

In 1993 there was Dave Parmenter's classic "The Land That Duke Forgot," in which the renowned surfer/shaper/writer/curmudgeon turned his caustic wit (and exceptional powers of observation) on the frigid shores of Alaska, revealing the potential waiting above 45 degrees north latitude. Recent ice-water revelations like Norway, Nova Scotia, and Newfoundland (all capital Ns for numb nuts) owe their eventual appearances as destinations to this early Arctic adventure.

At the opposite end of the spectrum were the travel tales of prolific photographer and trailblazer John Callahan, who focused on the belt of warm water circling the globe. Philippine perfection at Cloud Nine, blue heaven in the Maldives, wild New Guinea, and the untouched Andaman Islands—the intrepid Callahan specialized in tropical discoveries in which his photo subjects left the first tracks . . . or at least brought home the first photos.

Not that SURFER can't keep a secret. Take the trip the footloose Aussie photographer Ted Grambeau took to the Atlantic island of Madeira in 1994. Ted had been given a tip by French surf journalist Gibus de Soltrait about the potential for big surf on this verdant, precipitous island lying just off the coast of Portugal. De Soltrait had traipsed along its crenelated coastline with a surfboard twenty years earlier but hadn't heard of a surfer visiting since. That was enough for SURFER senior editor Sam George, future editor Evan Slater, and Hawaiian haole Ross Williams, who followed Grambeau to that exotic isle, where they discovered world-class waves near an isolated village called Jardim do Mar. Much to George's later consternation, Grambeau insisted the name of the island not be used—and it wasn't. The resulting feature was eventually called "Garden by the Sea." Yet despite the ruse, Madeira almost immediately became a surf destination; European surfers, especially, proving more handy with their atlases than they had previously been given credit for.

SURFER's policy regarding surf-spot identification has always been in flux—placing Bali in the South Pacific no longer works in the Google Earth era. Moving into the new millennium, the general standard was to place the location on a map without drawing a map. But if this strategy worked, it was only to salve the conscience of SURFER editors and photographers—the surfer's voracious appetite for new fantasy surf would not be denied by mere subterfuge.

SURFER's readers, apparently, wouldn't have it any other way. More recent discoveries in Mexico, the Line Islands, Iceland, and Canada have inspired wanderlust in second- (and sometimes third-) generation SURFER devotees, but in every case the actual locations have been obscured. Gone are the days when surfers looked for traveling companions, and SURFER must shoulder much of the blame for that self-serving aesthetic. The ethical stance of a magazine that specializes in exposing new surf breaks while trying not to reveal their actual locations doesn't stand up to much scrutiny. But in most cases, it's SURFER's readers who have perpetuated this policy: An overwhelming majority continue to assert that they cherish their surf-travel fantasies even more than travel itself; the thrill of discovery, however contrived, is still the ultimate pleasure.

Can you blame them? Since the very first issue of *The Surfer* reached the hands of surfers desperate for affirmation and inspiration, its message has been crystal clear. It's not just about riding waves—it never has been. Like the waves themselves, we surfers seem destined to wander this earth searching for that most harmonious landfall. Whether perfection waits on the other side of the world or just up the highway matters little. Since that first issue, the object for most surfers has been "to seek and find the perfect day, the perfect wave, and be alone with the surf and [their] thoughts."
—SG

THANKS IN LARGE PART TO *SURFER* MAGAZINE'S FIFTY-YEAR HISTORY OF SPONSORING GLOBAL SURF EXPLORATION, THE FIRST FOREIGNERS ENCOUNTERED BY MANY INDIGENOUS COASTAL CULTURES HAVE BEEN SURFERS. ILHA DAS ROLAS ISLANDER CHUM (LEFT) AND SAM GEORGE. 2007.

❶ LIKE MODERN ROCK CLIMBERS WHO FOLLOW THE ROUTES OF THEIR PIONEERING PREDECESSORS WITHOUT ROPES, TODAY'S TOP SURFERS PLAY IN WAVES THAT THEIR DISCOVERERS ONCE FEARED. **KELLY SLATER**, MENTAWAI, INDONESIA. ❷ IN THE EARLY '60S, ADVENTURE STILL LAY WITHIN A HALF TANK OF GAS. VENTURA OVERHEAD. ❸ THE UBIQUITOUS *PANGA* SKIFF HAS BECOME THE EXPLORATION VEHICLE OF CHOICE IN MANY TROPICAL LATITUDES. ❹ AUSTRALIA'S INTREPID PROTO-TRAVELER **PETER TROY** POSED FOR A SET-UP PHOTO THAT WAS ACTUALLY SHOT OUT BEHIND THE *SURFER* OFFICES IN CAPISTRANO BEACH. ❺ STRANGERS IN A STRANGE LAND—AND A '57 KOMBI. AN EVOCATIVE DETAIL OF **RON PERROTT'S** 1966 SOUTH AFRICAN SURFARI. ❻ IN THE LATE 1980S, SURF-TRAVEL COMPANIES BEGAN PACKAGING *SURFER'S* MONTHLY FANTASY OFFERINGS. **SEAN MURPHY**, OWNER OF WATERWAYS TRAVEL, ENJOYING HIS JOB IN TIMOR, INDONESIA.

"THERE ARE PLACES IN THE WORLD THAT PUMP PERFECT WAVES THAT NOBODY SURFS BUT THEY ALL REQUIRE SOME DEGREE OF HASSLE TO GET TO, AND ANY SUCH VENTURE IS ALWAYS A GAMBLE . . . BUT IN MY OPINION THE ANSWER TO THE DEPRESSED LOCAL WHO IS INSPIRED BY AN OLD SURFER'S PICTURES OF SOME OTHER PLACE IS: STAY AT HOME AND IN REALITY."

MICHAEL BARAN
FROM "TEN SPOTS YOU'LL PROBABLY NEVER SURF," SEPTEMBER 1973

opposite: THE INTREPID MS. LIZ CLARK. DISPATCHES FROM HER INTREPID SOLO CIRCUMNAVIGATION, RUN PERIODICALLY IN *SURFER*, HELPED KEEP THE SPIRIT OF CLASSIC SURF ADVENTURE ALIVE. VSLANDS.

PROTECTING THE GUILTY

BY STEVE PEZMAN

RON STONER'S '65 FORD COMET WAS BRAND NEW WHEN HE LOADED IT UP WITH PERIOD SURF STARS AND POINTED IT SOUTH OF THE BORDER TO MAZATLÁN. BY THE TIME IT GOT BACK THE STATION WAGON—AND THE SURFING WORLD—WOULD NEVER BE THE SAME.

TO SURF IS TO TRAVEL. I KNEW THAT LONG BEFORE I SAT AT THE EDITOR'S DESK AT *SURFER*.

In 1960, five of my buddies and I loaded into my 1951 Plymouth and drove to Mazatlán, Mexico. I had twenty-five dollars in my pocket—the others had about the same. It took us three days, including one breakdown just north of Culiacán, where the ingenious local mechanics somehow adapted Fiat brushes to fit my worn-out generator. When we finally arrived in Mazatlán, we felt we had traveled beyond the known universe into another reality—one with surf, at a time when riding waves was all but unknown beyond a few Southern California beach towns. But when we pulled up at Lupe's Loopers north of town, feeling so gnarly and far-flung, there on the beach was almost everyone we knew from Seal Beach Pier! Unbeknownst to us, they had driven down before we did. Shit! But the crowd of hometown heroes notwithstanding, we did score some incredible waves.

Imagine our surprise when in 1966 SURFER ran an extensive feature on a Ron Stoner trip to mainland Mexico, in which editor John Severson outrageously renamed our fabulous Matanchen Bay discovery "Stoner's Point" in honor of his star photographer who had supposedly "discovered" the break. The article featured Tom Lenardo, Bill Fury, and Jack Cantu, all of whom we knew and liked. So we weren't that pissed off; we were more amused.

The world seemed much larger then. In the mid-1960s I shipped out in the merchant marine on a freighter carrying a PX cargo of 8,600 tons of stale Hamm's and Schlitz beer from San Francisco to Hawaii, Guam, the Philippines, then Viet-Nam, and carrying servicemen's cars home from Japan on the return voyage. Little did I realize at the time that there was rideable surf in every country I visited.

In 1967, Australian Peter Troy came traipsing through California, having previously spread the seeds of surfing in countries like Brazil and France during his epic round-the-world adventure—really the first of its kind. Troy hung out with Severson for a few weeks, and I shaped him a tri-plane surfboard without ever meeting him. The truth was, in the early 1970s we still had a provincial view of the surfing world. We knew the Southern California coastline had waves, at least from San Francisco to Cuatro Casas, in Baja, and in the Mazatlán area of the mainland. Photos of Australian surf by Ron Perrott and Jack Eden had appeared in SURFER. We had heard of Peru and knew its east coast had waves of a sort; but by and large, outside of Hawaii and our home grounds, the surfing life seemed exclusive to our own little world. That naive bubble would soon burst.

After an apprenticeship that seemed to last only weeks in 1971, I took my place in the pantheon of SURFER editors. Not long afterward, I began running stories by a pair of intrepid young Orange County surfers, Craig Peterson and Kevin Naughton. While travel had long been standard fare in SURFER's pages, these guys were the sport's first true surf-travel savants. The world of waves was opening like a blossom, and Naughton-Peterson, as they came to be known, were out there on the cutting edge of dirt-bag exploration. Their travel features remain some of the most memorable and popular articles ever run in SURFER. But not with everyone, as I would soon learn.

When the duo eventually emerged from their first extended Central American trip with startling shots of an outrageous beachbreak in mainland Mexico, we ran a rare nonaction cover shot. The composition was perfect. In the foreground, some of their gear hung from a driftwood limb in the sand; in the center were the two surfers with a beautiful, unridden wave peeling off in shades of gray and green in the background. The cover blurb read, "Discovery on the Way Home from Central America!" That classic cover fired up more than just imaginations.

It turns out the break was the legendary Petacalco, now extinct due to a hydroelectric dam that eventually choked off the littoral sand flow that created its epic peaks. But little did I know that our cover story had exposed more than just Mexico's potential for world-class big waves. It also had blown the lid off one of surfing's great secrets: a cabal of deeply embedded hardcore Laguna Beach/San Diego guys who, after much laborious travel exploration—and an almost paranoid aversion to publicity of any sort—had planted their flag there, riding some of the world's deepest barrels in total obscurity.

I clearly remember when, soon after the issue had hit the stands, SURFER receptionist extraordinaire Shirley Ziegler (who could remember the name attached to a voice on the phone a year after a single call) buzzed me on Sevo's old intercom.

"Some gentlemen here to see you," she said in deadpan. I asked her to send them back. Into my office stormed three enraged surfers, including Laguna's Pat Tobin and Pierre Michel, furiously brandishing in my face the offending issue of SURFER.

"How could you do this?" they scolded. "We worked so hard to find that wave, and you blow it off to sell magazines for money!"

I have to admit that this argument had not previously surfaced. I was a bit taken aback, because

I felt that up to that point in my editorial tenure I'd maintained a vestige of soul while converting the actual surfing life into colored dots on paper. I tried to reason with the trio, who were growing ever more livid, making the argument that I hadn't really hurt anything: The article included no place names, no maps. And besides, in sixty days a new issue would come out, the article would soon be forgotten, and their surf break would recede back into anonymity.

They scoffed at this. "Nothing goes back the way it was," they said ruefully. I offered up my final defense: They were lucky I was in the publisher's chair. At least I would listen to them and could even relate to what they were saying. I'd seen an exotic surf spot we'd once enjoyed on our own, a surf spot that, by dint of the ordeal involved in its discovery, we felt a certain entitlement to, exposed in the pages of SURFER. I knew what came next. And at least I cared enough to be contrite. This desperate point of order finally succeeded in diminishing their tirade into a mere

(and infinitely more manageable) heated discussion, although they did leave still shaking their fists. We all later became friends, however.

But that meeting changed SURFER forever. For future SURFER editors, dealing with travel destinations—to spell it all out or not—would never be as simple as it had been before that episode. In a recent issue of SURFER, I noticed a travel story about a certain South Pacific island in the Gilbert Chain. As publisher of the *Surfer's Journal*, I had previously run photos and even a feature on this island, clearly identifying the idyllic spot. In SURFER, however, its Gilbertese name was jumbled—deliberately I assume—to protect the guilty. The atoll has no local surfers, no cloistered, paranoid surf colonists—no reason, really, to obscure its true location. But the point made so emphatically in my office thirty-five years ago has long since become policy.

"WE WORKED SO HARD TO FIND THAT WAVE, AND YOU BLOW IT OFF TO SELL MAGAZINES FOR MONEY!"

surfer

CDCw
00568

VOLUME FOURTEEN · NUMBER FIVE · JANUARY · ONE DOLLAR

Discovery on the way home from Central America

SETTING THE MOOD: THAT FLORIDIAN BOB ROTHERHAM ISN'T EVEN LOOKING AT THE
BACKGROUND DREAM WAVE MADE THIS THE MOST POWERFUL *SURFER* TRAVEL COVER EVER.

OFF THE MAP

In the Victorian Era, explorers would return from
darkest Africa or the icy wastes of the South Pole to
present their findings to the Royal Geographic Society in London. During the Golden Age of Surf Exploration in the early 1970s, the equivalent honor was
having an article run in SURFER. One of the sport's
most intrepid surf explorers is Hawaii's Randy
Rarick, who in 1972 embarked on a remarkable overland trip along the west coast of southern Africa.
Rarick, Peter French, and Brian Hinde, in a second-
hand Land Rover, got to Cape Town and turned right,
leaving a surfer's first tracks through the remote
Namib Desert and on the previously unridden waves
of Angola. The resulting SURFER article featured
no images of their adventures, however; associate
editor Kurt Ledterman decided against running any
photos of their surf discoveries, preferring to let the
reader's imagination fill in the story beyond epic
travel shots like this one, taken at a remote *farol*
(lighthouse) somewhere along the Angolan coast. ▬

COLONIAL SURF

When in 1987 SURFER writer/photographer Matt George first hiked along Bali's Bukit Peninsula, the name "Bingin" was still whispered, the closest thing to a secret spot on an island that had already seen more than a decade of surf tourism. Twenty-three years after that first account (which disclosed no actual location), the sleepy beach at Bingin has been transformed into another Surf City, an entire cottage industry having sprung up around the foreigners drawn to its user-friendly left bowl. It's a pattern of colonization repeated around the globe: El Salvador, Costa Rica, Sumatra, the Philippines, Nicaragua, Madeira, Puerto Rico, Morocco. All these exotic surf zones debuted in the pages of SURFER, and the culture of every one of them changed as a result. For the better? Heedless surfers helped turned the once-idyllic village of Lagundri Bay on the Sumatran island of Nias into a seaside Sodom and Gomorrah. At the same time, the infant mortality rate at Bali's Uluwatu, the once-lonely outpost now a prosperous tourist destination, has dropped to next to nothing. The yin and yang of surf travel articles—change sometimes for the better, sometimes for the worse, but always change. ▬

❶ LAND ROVIN' THROUGH ANGOLA, 1972. ❷ BALINESE BOOMTOWN AT BINGIN, 2009. ❸ IN 2003, *SURFER* PHOTO EDITOR **JASON MURRAY** AND FRIENDS DISCOVERED THIS BAJA JEWEL RIGHT UNDER THE NOSES OF AT LEAST FORTY YEARS' WORTH OF MEXICAN SURF EXPLORERS.

THE FIRST RESORT

There had been surf camps before, Grajagen in Java most notably, but those were mostly treehouses and hammocks with a view. But when Tavara Island Resort opened for business in 1984, it introduced the slightly shocking concept of the surf resort, complete with private bungalows, showers, catered meals, and boat rides out to the reef. And while the initial $100-a-night tariff seemed outrageous to most surfers at the time ("Are you kidding? I could last a month in Baja for that!"), the benefits of paying to play quickly became obvious with every new SURFER spread on the Fijian paradise. ▬

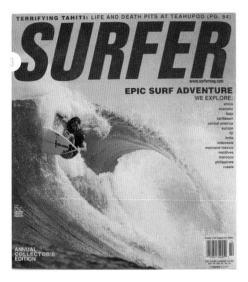

DON'T ASK; DON'T TELL

The ongoing strategy of obscuring the actual locations of newly discovered surf spots worked only to salve the conscience of SURFER editors and photographers—surfers' voracious appetites for new fantasy surf would not be denied by mere subterfuge. In October 2000, SURFER's annual "Big Issue" was dedicated exclusively to travel and exploration. The cover featured Dan Malloy riding a previously undocumented Caroline Islands reef pass. The accompanying feature by former SURFER photo editor Rob Gilley revealed one more epic surf discovery, fulfilling all the standard criteria: hollow tropical barrels, only a couple of surfers out, gorgeous island backdrop. Was the particular island named? Of course not—Gilley wouldn't hear of it. Gilley's story of being tipped off by his dentist as to this "lost" island's latitude and longitude made good copy, but in actuality the SURFER crew was hosted by a gracious American expat while at the same time a visiting Brazilian was establishing a surf camp. In the years since, the P-Pass surf resort has been up and running full tilt, hosting a number of high-profile clients including Shane Dorian, Andy Irons, and Kelly Slater—the latter two even filming a surf movie segment there in 2008. And to this day, the island has never been named in SURFER magazine.

1 WEST AUSTRALIA DESERT RIG. **2** SHANE DORIAN, TAVARUA RIGHTS. **3** GILLEY'S "NOT-SO-SECRET-SPOT" COVER.
4 G-LAND HAMMOCK-WITH-A-VIEW. **5** DAVE RASTOVICH, MENTAWAI ISLANDS.

1 PANAITAN ISLAND, WEST JAVA. 2 (LEFT-RIGHT) TIMMY TURNER, TRAVIS POTTER, NYOMAN, BRETT SCHWARTZ. 3 TIMMY TURNER, WEST JAVA.

TURNING FERAL

In 2002, SURFER reader were treated to an extraordinary travel feature that was more than just a throwback to the Golden Era of dirt-bag surf adventure. Call it the Anti-Boat Trip. By the new millennium, most travel stories had taken on a uniform template: a team of sponsored professional surfers being toured around some exotic surf location—most often Sumatra's Mentawai Islands—on increasingly luxurious boat excursions. The hermetically sealed boat trip assured a uniformity in imagery that helped fuel a multimillion-dollar surf-charter industry (the obligatory lineup with skiff in foreground, the jumping-off-the-top-deck shot, the après surf beer-and-grommet head-shaving debacle). But readers couldn't help but become a bit more jaded by each issue's monthly carnival cruise. Enter Huntington Beach's Timmy Turner and his feral cohorts Travis Potter and Brett Schwartz. Dropping way off the editorial pro's fast track, these former NSSA stars chose to pack a duffle, heft a bag of rice, and disappear into the remote reaches of Indonesia, traveling overland, beach camping, and generally sweating and swatting their way through the Eastern monsoon, all for a few epic barrels. And we mean truly epic, documented by Indo vet Jason Childs and filmed by auteur Turner himself for his quite remarkable film *Second Thoughts*. When it came to modern surf adventure, this was the real deal, headless chickens and all. Somewhere Peter Troy was smiling.

FOLLOW
THAT WAVE

BY KEVIN NAUGHTON

HOW FAR WILL YOU
FOLLOW THAT WAVE?
IN YOUR ANSWER
LIVES A SURF
ADVENTURE.

The taproot of all adventure is *the need to find out*. That's what sends surfers wandering, chasing waves to the most remote locations on the planet. This shared motivation of finding waves is our common bond, transcending borders and nationalities. We all start at our home breaks and expand outward, exploring the next county, then the next country, and on to the next continent. Along the way, we see the world, and the world, in turn, has an endless-summer image of us: boards under arms, eyes squinting seaward, checking the surf. What is it about waves that makes travelers of us all?

When Craig Peterson and I hit the road on our own surf quest in the early '70s, the global surf trail was an unmarked path on a secret map buried in the sand of beaches without footprints. The known destinations could be counted on two hands (with one hand holding the wax!): Jeffreys, Tamarin Bay, La Barre. The yet-to-be-discovered places: Indo, Southern Mex, Central America, Fiji—the list goes on and on—were still in the coconut wireless stages of secrecy. Before the magazines suddenly discover a spot, rumors of its whereabouts have drifted like smoke 'round campfires the world over.

Both Craig and I had the necessary traits for survival in strange lands: We were young and clueless. Age and experience slow you down

KEVIN NAUGHTON

BOAT TRIP **NAUGHTON/PETERSON** STYLE, EN ROUTE TO WEST AFRICA, CIRCA 1975.

and make you cautious. Sometimes it really is better not to know any better. How else could you explain two surfers, sixteen and eighteen, loading a couple of surfboards onto a battered VW and saying, "Hey, let's go check the waves in Central America!" No sponsors, no travel expenses, no surf forecasts or itinerary to speak of. We just packed up and hit the road.

Craig had been cutting his teeth as an up-and-coming surf photographer in the Newport/Huntington area, and I was doing the same as a surfer at the Huntington Beach pier. Craig heard that I'd already been to Southern France and El Salvador and that I was ready to leave for Central America. We shared a common interest: finding waves no other surfers had seen. Craig finagled a few dozen rolls of film from SURFER, which was a big deal in those days. The reaction to our travel plans at the magazine might've been, "Who are these crazy dudes?" Instead, they said, "Central America? Uh, sure, go for it!" Off we went, on our first foray as "SURFER travel correspondents."

SURFER was the main conduit for events flowing through the surf world. In the '60s, it was *the* source for surf adventures. The articles that stuck with me were the travel pieces to South Africa, Mauritius, San Blas, and other faraway places. My hero was an unprepossessing surfer sitting by the side of the road with his board, hitching a ride to somewhere; Australian Peter Troy embodied the ideal of the lone surfer on an adventure. A backpack, board, and searching eye were all one needed to follow in his footsteps.

Surfers in the '60s and '70s were picking up where the '50s Beat generation had left off. Like Jack Kerouac's intrepid travelers, surf travelers occupied the fringes of society; our shortboards and long hair exiled us from Main Street. Instead of roaming America in search of its beat, we headed to places unknown, following a different drummer.

When we arrived in El Salvador in 1972, La Libertad and El Zunzal were the kinds of places surfers dream about: great waves, friendly locals, cheap living, and only a few others to share it with. Like a lot of the best things in life, we took it all for granted, imagining it would always remain this way.

In El Salvador, one month passed, then two blurred into three while the waves kept coming. Craig took the pics, and at a candle-lit table cluttered with bottles of Tic-Tac (the local firewater), we recounted our adventures and mailed them off to the States in envelopes plastered with exotic-looking stamps. At the SURFER office, the photo editor opened one of our film canisters and a large wasp flew out, angrily buzzing the photo room and causing the staff to flee for cover. They ran the story anyway, along with photos that blew the surfing world away with the possibilities that were out there. Meanwhile, we were miring the VW in the sand at beaches across Costa Rica on our "further adventures." By the time we returned home, even the scrap dealers wouldn't look at the VW—as if it mattered. SURFER had taken the unprecedented step of running a third installment, the simple cover story: "Discovery on the Way Home from Central America."

When Craig's photos of big perfect waves in deep Mexico ran, surfers reacted like a school of stunned mullets; it was a surfing epiphany that waves of this size and quality could be found simply by chance. The traveling bug had bitten the surfing world, with symptoms being manifested in surfers throughout the United States, at least, who began rethinking their plans for the immediate future. The only apparent cure was to put careers, schools, marriages, and all the usual baggage of life on hold and head south for a taste of adventure wrapped in a tortilla.

The magazine was surprised by the popular responses to our everyman-goes-looking-for-waves misadventures, and they asked us where we wanted to go to next.

BY IMMERSING OURSELVES IN THE PLACES WE TRAVELED TO, WE SAW THAT THE MOST INTERESTING THINGS ON A SURF TRIP HAPPEN OUTSIDE THE SURF.

Craig and I gave the globe a spin. When it stopped, we were looking at the west coast of Africa, from Morocco through the Sahara Desert and all the way to the Congo. From a surf-traveler's point of view, it was all unexplored. Again, inexperience and luck were on our side. In travel—as in life—it's better to be lucky than rich. SURFER gave us just enough coin to get us going, but not enough to get back home. It was either a comment on our traveling prowess or a way to get rid of us.

Nine months later, we'd covered a big chunk of west Africa, Morocco, Europe, the Azores, and the Caribbean, and we returned home by third-class bus via Central America and Mexico. We'd hit our stride and acquired that most ephemeral of all traits: a feel for the road. The editorial assistant at SURFER, Chris Maxwell, was in charge of typing up our dispatches, which had been written with leaky pens, often in the backs of buses, on whatever paper we could find in west Africa. She told us later that the staff knew they had a good piece on their hands when they heard her laughing as she transcribed. Through the pages of SURFER, we'd taken the surfing world with us on misadventures halfway around the world, with waves and wild times as our personal payoff.

Any surfer worth his surf wax was either going somewhere or had a trip planned, and many of them attributed that travel stoke to our stories in SURFER. Look—with all the things that went wrong on our travels, if we could survive and have fun, so could everyone else! By coincidence, many early surf destinations later became world-class tourist hot spots: Bali, Hossegor, Mauritius, and Jeffreys Bay to name a few. Surfers were the first ones there, camping out or living on the cheap.

More trips and articles followed. Back to Africa to explore the coastline of the Spanish Sahara, Europe in the off-season, and then Fiji for a piece on a new twist in the surfer's list of places to go: Tavarua surf camp. More than a decade had passed since our first articles ran in SURFER. Tavarua would be a turning point in the concept of surf travel, a location suited to surfers who had only a week or two, rather than a few months, to find waves and wanted to make the best of a short trip.

Once you get the travel bug in your veins, it's a happy virus that never goes away. Surfers are always looking forward to their next wave. To find that wave on an adventure is still the best trip going, and it carries from generation to generation. In 2002, I was on assignment to the Mentawais for SURFER, along with a few up-and-coming pros. I had to smile because although none of them recognized me, their fathers knew who I was.

For many, the '70s will go down as the era of surf adventures. But if you think the glory days of surf travel are over, just look at a globe. What you see is a lifetime of coastlines surrounded by oceans of possibilities.

Drop a pebble in a still pool . . . watch the waves radiate outward and consider this: You are that pebble, the still pool is the world of waves. The question is: How far will you follow that wave? In your answer lives a surf adventure.

opposite: CLASSIC **NAUGHTON/PETERSON** FARE: THE TRAVAILS OF OVERLAND AFRICAN ADVENTURE, THE PAYOFF IN PREVIOUSLY UNRIDDEN EXOTICA.

TOP 10 FANTASY WAVE REVELATIONS

(ARRANGE IN ORDER ACCORDING TO ONE'S SURFING ABILITIES; RESISTANCE TO REEF RASH, MALARIA, AND FROSTBITE; AND WHETHER YOU RIDE GOOFY OR REGULAR.)

JEFFREYS BAY. IN *SURFER*'S FIRST MODERN SURF-TRIP FEATURE, PHOTOGRAPHER RON PERROTT AND HIS CREW OF PERIPATETIC AUSSIES NOT ONLY REVEALED SOUTH AFRICA'S TRUE POINTBREAK POTENTIAL (BEYOND *ENDLESS SUMMER*'S CAPE ST. FRANCIS) BUT ALSO ESTABLISHED THE TEMPLATE FOR VIRTUALLY ALL TRAVEL ARTICLES TO COME.

SANTOSHA. THE BIG DADDY OF ALL TRAVEL FEATURES, THIS ARTICLE FOOLED EVEN THOSE WHO'D READ THE *SURFER* STORY ON MAURITIUS TEN YEARS EARLIER. THIS ONE HAD IT ALL: THE TRIPPY PSEUDONYM AND THE GRASS HUT ON THE EXOTIC SHORE; BUT MORE IMPORTANT, THE TROPICAL HOLLOW DANGER-LEFT—A GOLD STANDARD IN FANTASY SURF THAT HAS ENDURED FOR TWENTY-FIVE YEARS.

HOSSEGOR. SET WITHIN A BROADER STORY ABOUT A SURF TRIP TO THE SOUTH OF FRANCE FOR THE FILMING OF MACGILLIVRAY/FREEMAN'S *WAVES OF CHANGE*, THE BIG REVEAL WAS THAT A SHORT DRIVE UP THE COAST FROM THE RESORT BEACHES OF BIARRITZ LAY UNTRAMMELED BEACHBREAK PERFECTION. GROUND ZERO FOR EUROPE'S SURF BOOM.

STONER'S POINT. PUBLISHED ONLY TWO ISSUES AFTER PERROTT'S AFRICAN ADVENTURE, THIS CHRONICLE OF *SURFER*'S ACE LENSMAN RON STONER'S MEXICAN ODYSSEY (IN A MERCURY COMET, NO LESS) ADDED THE TWO FINISHING TOUCHES TO THE MODERN TRAVEL STORY: AN ACCOMPANYING TEAM OF CONTEMPORARY SURF STARS AND THE NOW-UBIQUITOUS SURF-SPOT PSEUDONYM.

LAGUNDRI BAY. BUT WE ALL CALLED IT "NIAS." SURE, JUST MORE INDONESIAN PERFECTION, AND PERHAPS THE GREATEST SINGLE TRAVEL LINEUP EVER TAKEN (BY ERIK AEDER). BUT MORE IMPORTANTLY, IT OPENED THE DOOR TO THE ISLANDS OF WESTERN SUMATRA AND THE MENTAWAI MOTHER LODE.

ULUWATU. OKAY, SO THEY GOT IT WRONG AND SAID BALI WAS IN THE SOUTH PACIFIC. STILL, THIS FIRST LOOK AT THE INDONESIAN ARCHIPELAGO, IN 1975, WOULD EVENTUALLY ADD MORE WATERY REAL ESTATE TO THE GLOBAL SURF MAP THAN ANY OTHER *SURFER* STORY. NEXT CAME PADANG-PADANG, THEN G-LAND, THEN . . .

MADEIRA. LOCATED ONLY AN HOUR OR SO WEST OF THE WELL-SURFED PORTUGUESE COAST, THE ATLANTIC ISLAND OF MADEIRA HAD BEEN SURF-EXPLORED ONLY ONCE BEFORE A *SURFER* TEAM LANDED THERE IN 1995. THIS WAS THE EQUIVALENT OF A GROUP OF BRAZILIANS COMING TO CALIFORNIA THE SAME YEAR AND DISCOVERING THE RANCH.

PETACALCO. OF COURSE IT WASN'T CALLED "PETACALCO." PART THREE IN THE NAUGHTON-PETERSON TRAVEL TRIPTYCH (FOLLOWING EL SALVADOR AND COSTA RICA), THIS INSTALLMENT, WITH ITS SUBLIME COVER SHOT AND STAGGERING ERIC PENNY SPREAD, WAS A REVELATION. AS THE CAPTION READ: "15 TO 18 FEET . . . AND IT AIN'T HAWAII."

CLOUD NINE. RANDY RARICK, SURFING'S SIR FRANCIS DRAKE, HAD BEEN TO THE PHILIPPINES BACK IN THE '70s, DISCOVERING MUGGY SHOREBREAK THAT RAISED NO PULSES. SO WHEN IN 1993 THE INTREPID PHOTOGRAPHER JOHN CALLAHAN REVEALED THIS FLAWLESS SLICE OF FILIPINO REEF—RIDDEN BY TAYLOR KNOX AND FUTURE EDITOR EVAN SLATER—AN ENTIRELY NEW INTERNATIONAL SURFING CULTURE WAS BORN.

ALASKA/ICELAND. THESE TWO ARCTIC EXPEDITIONS HAVE TO BE LUMPED TOGETHER. WHILE THEY HAPPENED SEVERAL YEARS APART—'93 AND '97—THEY MADE A SINGULAR STATEMENT: "THERE'S SURF IN THEM THAR ICEBERGS!" BOTH DISCOVERIES COMPLETELY RECONFIGURED OUR PERCEPTION OF THE GLOBE. HAVING BEEN WRITTEN BY RESPECTED SURF LAUREATES DAVE PARMENTER AND DANIEL DUANE , RESPECTIVELY, DIDN'T HURT EITHER.

TOP 5

WHAT TOOK YOU SO LONG?

1. **THE MENTAWAIS.** C'MON YOU GUYS! ERIK AEDER BROKE THE SUMATRA STORY IN 1975, FOR CRYIN' OUT LOUD! SO WHY DID IT TAKE ANOTHER TWENTY-ONE YEARS UNTIL THE FIRST MACARONIS SHOTS (TOM CURREN, BROCK LITTLE, AND SHEA LOPEZ WITH SONNY MILLER) HIT THE STANDS?

2. **BARRA DE LA CRUZ.** OKAY, PUERTO ESCONDIDO IS A TOUGH ACT TO FOLLOW. BUT CONSIDERING THAT TUNED-IN MEX-TRAVELERS HAD BEEN TRAIPSING DOWN TO THIS SOUTHERN POINT FOR AT LEAST A DECADE BEFORE IT WENT PUBLIC IN THE NEW MILLENNIUM, IT'S AMAZING NOBODY THOUGHT TO BRING A CAMERA SOONER.

3. **P-PASS.** A COVER STORY IN *SURFER*'S 2002 "BIG ISSUE," THIS REEF PASS IN THE CAROLINE ISLANDS STILL ISN'T CALLED BY ITS PROPER NAME, DESPITE THE FACT THAT THERE'S A SURF RESORT THERE NOW CATERING TO THE LIKES OF SLATER, IRONS, AND DORIAN. AND YET *SURFER* EDITOR SAM GEORGE HAD BEEN TOLD ABOUT IT ALMOST A DECADE BEFORE THE STORY APPEARED. WHAT'S WITH THAT?

4. **PUERTO RICO.** THAT'S RIGHT, PUERTO RICO. SURE, THEY HAD THE WORLD CONTEST THERE IN 1968. SO WHY DID IT TAKE SURFERS—AND SURFER PHOTOGRAPHERS—MORE THAN THIRTY YEARS TO EXPLORE THE COASTLINE BETWEEN AGUADILLA AND SAN JUAN? WHO KNEW THAT PLACE HAD BARRELS?

5. **PUNTA LOBOS.** *SURFER* RAN STORIES ON SOUTH AMERICAN SURFING AS FAR BACK AS 1961. WHAT, THEY COULDN'T DRAG THEMSELVES AWAY FROM CLUB WAIKIKI IN LIMA, PERU, TO CHECK OUT THE COASTLINE TO THE SOUTH? THE FACT THAT DECADES PASSED BEFORE CHILE'S LAND O' LEFTS—INCLUDING THE INCOMPARABLE PUNTA LOBOS—WAS REVEALED SIMPLY BOGGLES THE MIND.

A CHARTERED VAGABOND

BY STEVE BARILOTTI

I BEGAN TO WONDER IF IN THIS INCREASINGLY GENERIC MCTRAVELWORLD THERE WERE STILL PLACES UNSURFED AND AS WILD AS I HAD FANTASIZED OVER SINCE I STARTED READING THE MAGS.

I was at midcrossing in the Banyuwangi channel when I realized I'd run away and joined the circus for good.

Dark. A warm, wet breeze blowing across the narrow straits separating Bali from Java. Aboard a rusty, Indonesian car ferry chugging along at eleven knots. The sweet, exotic incense of a clove *kretek* wafted from the wheelhouse above. The whole scene had the corrupted tropical ambience of a Conrad novella, save for the muffled electronic chatter of a big-screen TV echoing from the ferry's main lounge. The first match of the State of Origin rugby championships was on that week. Periodically, I would hear rude yelps and drunken Australian curses burst over the low diesel-engine thrum. Sizable bets worth millions of Indonesian rupiah were riding on this game.

I was alone at the rail taking in the Southern Cross and the phosphorescence arcing off the ferry's bow wake. Every now and again I'd spot the small firefly lantern of a *prahu* outrigger fisherman daring the treacherous currents and

the deadly green goddess who lurks just below the seemingly placid waters of the Bali Straits. Had we run one down, I doubt our progress would have slowed a second.

Late May, 1995: I was en route with the ASP Top 44 as a media-camp follower to Java's far eastern edge for the inaugural Quiksilver G-Land Pro. This was a touchstone moment: my first fully expense-paid assignment to one of the marquee left-hand breaks of the planet. The plane ticket and hotel vouchers had arrived special-delivery from HQ as if I were a war correspondent sent to cover a late-breaking banana-republic coup.

Like most Faustian bargains, not quite as I imagined—but certainly what I'd prayed for a few years earlier while line editing SURFER magazine copy at the Dana Point offices. It had been eight years since I'd sold my first spec piece to SURFER, five since I had been brought on as a salaried, in-house editor, and three since I had been laid off and reverted to full-time freelancing. In the interim, I'd paid my dues writing countless utility columns, and the natural attrition due to the mortgages, marriages, and child-rearing of my peers moved me up the magazine-travel food chain. Now in my midthirties I was an aging lost boy on the ship to Pleasure Island to play pirates with the Top 44 and their handlers.

Most of the pros had spent the week's lead-up in Bali surfing Uluwatu and the Bukit and partying at Tubes bar and the Sari Club (later to gain infamy as Ground Zero of the 2002 Bali bombings). Late every night they would be poured onto a tour bus and spirited through the teak plantation villages with a motorcycle escort, hazard lights flashing. Most were sleeping off the vicious hangover generated by the Sari's notorious "Arak Attack." A goodly number were still tripping on mushrooms or Ecstasy. All in all, a restrained version of *Fear and Loathing*, or white men behaving badly in the tropics with the cameras rolling.

Truth be told, I was using the ASP pro tour as subterfuge to get into full-time travel-surf journalism—my dream since I'd first started reading the exploits of Naughton and Peterson in the mid-'70s. This ploy wasn't the greatest fit. I had little interest in competitive surfing or in trailing after rather conventional middle-class young men ten years my junior who were amazing surf athletes but were generally uninterested in much outside their well-insulated, if international, culture bubble. Not that I begrudged them their fun, but I always felt like a bit of a lurker sidling up to these guys at the competitor's tent hoping for a golden insight into why they had been so coldly underscored on their last ride.

But when the golden ticket finally arrived to visit the storied surf lands of Bali, I signed on, no questions asked.

My one-time editor Paul Holmes once asked me, "Why do you want to travel so much? Everywhere has become like everywhere else."

He had a point. In the wake of free-trade agreements and ramped-up globalization in the late twentieth century, the multinational corporations had bequeathed us a very sanitary and deadly boring version of the future. Mall culture had pervaded to the core of ancient cultures, and in the place of the alien, mysterious other, a modern-day Marco Polo encountered the franchised New World of Euro Starbucks, Kentucky Fried Chicken, and ubiquitous BP petrol stations selling embalmed Nestlé foodlike substances.

The surf universe, long on the outer fringe of pioneer tourism, had not escaped the flattening impact of a wired global village. As I picked up surfing's Silk Road in the early 1990s, I began to note a recurring, often depressing theme of surf neocolonialism. The list of one-time wave Shangri-la's turned surf ghettos—Kuta Beach, Jeffreys Bay, Nias, Hossegor, Puerto Escondido—was growing predictably longer. I began to wonder if in this increasingly generic McTravel world there were still places unsurfed and as wild as I had fantasized since I'd started reading the mags. And whether real adventure—or misadventure—still existed.

Even Grajagan, the mythic jungle of the late '70s, could be booked from a menu of Indonesian surf packages back in Kuta. Instead of a tiger-infested outpost, I found a basic but comfy boy's fort, complete with a stocked beer cooler, spaghetti Bolognese, and a big-screen TV playing a bootleg copy of *Pulp Fiction* each night. The contest organizers had set up a bank of Bose speakers on the beach near Bobby's Camp to pump out Pink Floyd's "Dark Side of the Moon" across the low-tide reef at sunset.

Still, I had to admit I was a long way from the basement of Safeco Title Insurance Company back in San Diego.

I was late to the surfing life. Through inauspicious birth I was raised 55 long, hot, smoggy miles from the ocean in Ontario, California. But a basement cafetorium showing of *Endless Summer* one afternoon by the nuns of St. George Parochial lit a secret seditious fire in me that soon manifested as a joyous middle finger extended toward long division and cursive penmanship. One day, I knew, I would be a surfer and ride that same cable car that soared Hynson and August to the top of Table Mountain in November 1963.

Shortly after high school graduation, I began surfing on the rural beaches north of Santa Barbara. As a despised kook beginner during surfing's mid-'70s Dark Ages of black-only wetsuits and virulent localism, I didn't have the benefit of leashes, surf schools, or long-range Internet forecasts. But in spite of Santa Barbara's legendary flat spells, I persevered and eventually parsed out a functional take-off and bottom turn. I devoured the surf mags promiscuously and made a nuisance of myself fondling new boards and wetsuits at the tiny Surf 'n Wear shop on Carrillo Street.

STEVE BARILOTTI

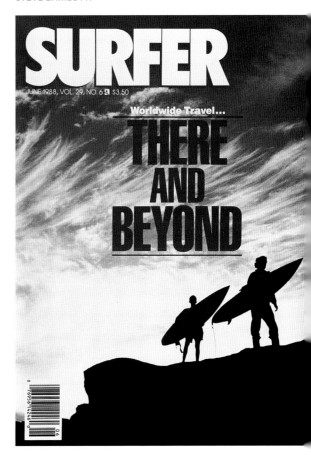

A PERENNIAL HIT: THE *SURFER* TRAVEL ISSUE.

But while I idolized the surfing of Gerry Lopez and Shaun Tomson and aspired to one day challenge the North Shore, what really fired my stoke were the rat-bag exploits of globe-trotting surf adventurers Kevin Naughton and Craig Peterson. I followed their capers, low-level scams, and occasional golden-wave scores from the pig latitudes of the surf frontier—Central America, Ivory Coast, Mexican mainland. And I wondered just how one would ever swing a dream gig like that.

Fortune smiled a couple of years later when I insinuated myself aboard a 55-foot, double-ended motorsailer bound for Hawaii and the South Pacific. Fired with naive enthusiasm at my good luck, I wrote then-publisher Steve Pezman a florid three-page pitch on why SURFER should sponsor me for a nominal monthly sum to be their roving South Seas correspondent. Three months later when we cast off from San Pedro, I'd received no reply. None followed.

Six months later, after enduring seasickness, three storms, doldrums, a tyrannical skipper, near-mutiny, near-starvation, and a polite but nonnegotiable request by the Papeete *gendarmerie* to use my ongoing ticket, I found myself beached back in San Diego. I got a job as a real-estate records' researcher (ironically dubbed a "searcher"), and spent the next six years as a virtual copy guy marooned among the endless stacks. I surfed little as I drifted through various relationships and stillborn career starts.

By way of happy accident and a journalism degree, I found myself working at SURFER at the turn of the '90s. The Dream Gig. By now, however, I was married with a deposit down on a small condo that was to be our first step up the SoCal equity ladder. The first child was mandated within a year.

The ultimate irony was that although I was now working for Steve Pezman (who chuckled wickedly when I told him of my letter years earlier), my job consisted of endless deadlines and long days spent commuting 60 miles each way to write surf tips or edit blueline proofs in a

cluttered fluorescent-lit cubicle not much different than the one I left back at the title company. Travel was limited to Triple Crown coverage on the North Shore for a couple weeks each winter. Surfing suffered. I often found myself feigning illness or an unprecedented number of family funerals to catch a new swell filtering into Northern Baja.

When I asked one of the mag's premier freelance photographers who'd just returned from a remote chain of surf-rich Indonesian islands just how one got to go on these dream trips, his advice was brutally illuminating: "Quit your job . . . get divorced."

In spite of my best intentions, the universe opened once again. Following a severe surf-industry contraction in the early '90s, I found myself back freelancing; around the same time I did a realistic ledger account of what I truly wanted my life to be this time around. And when it came down to playing pirates versus home-ownership and fatherhood . . . well . . . hell.

So, added together it's been a decent run. During the last seventeen years I've filled three passports with arcane visas in the search for pristine, perfect-moment lineups and cobbled together an income by writing dispatches sent back to the mag via Amsterdam Laundromat faxes and sweltering incense-perfumed cyber-warungs.

And I learned that true adventure doesn't begin until something goes horribly wrong. In spite of the most dedicated attempts of Disney and other corporate-culture merchants to create a perfectly safe consumer utopia through myth-stealing, there are still large chunks of the world that exist beyond the Orange County surfburbia cordon. It's Out There where the uncomfortably real and often dangerous stuff happens that makes good telling in retrospect. Because in the end, the only thing we truly own are our stories.

Some highlights included dodging the fish yakuza in Japan, blundering into a religious gang war in the Spice Islands, risking malaria

with barefoot-surfing doctors in the Mentawais, barely escaping a Peruvian *carcel* for sparking up an ill-advised joint in a Cuzco discotheque, sailing on poaching patrol with vegan ecopirates off the Galapagos, and once finding myself laid up with a spasmed back and food poisoning in a flea-ridden Madagascar hotel that doubled as a brothel come dusk.

And occasionally surfing some empty, life-altering waves. All up, thirty surf countries across six continents—Central America to Sumba, Newfoundland, the Tuamotus, and even sharing a shark cage and bottle of decent Cape merlot with Naughton and Peterson in South Africa. The ribald and occasionally dark backstories they shared from their original travels assured me I'd made the right choice, despite the constant hard scratch and low pay as a professional freelance writer for a niche publication.

And I eventually rode that cable car to the top.

Twice.

following spread: BEGINNING IN THE EARLY 1990S, *SURFER* RAN A NUMBER OF FEATURES ON ALASKAN SURF-HUNTING TRIPS, TRIGGERING A VERITABLE "COLD RUSH" OF NORTHERN LATITUDE EXPLORATION.

"ALL WOULD BE WAGERED FOR THE FINAL HAND IN THIS GAME OF CHANCE. THE ODDS PREPOSTEROUS; THE POT A FORTUNE; THE PLAYERS FICKLE; THE ANTE ADVENTURE. 'DEAL THEM CARDS!'"

CRAIG PETERSON AND KEVIN NAUGHTON
"BENEATH THE AFRICAN SUN," JULY 1975

WHO WE WATCH:
SURFER ON SURFERS

PERSONS OF INTEREST

SURFING BUILDS CHARACTERS—AND IF THOSE CHARACTERS didn't provide enormous inspiration, then SURFER, from the first to the very latest issue, would be filled with nothing but pretty pictures of empty waves. Beautiful, perhaps, but ultimately distant and dispassionate. It's people who bring meaning to the wave, because life *is* a wave; every wave is a life. Riding both well is the embodiment of style. To ride through life with a vibrancy that draws directly from the act of riding a wave: balance, spontaneity, daring, judgment, courage, and timing. Always timing. To understand this—to know this—is the trick. It's the intangible yet oh-so-obvious thing that separates the barefoot adventurer from what legend Phil Edwards described as "the legions of the unjazzed." And it's the reason John Severson called his new publication *The Surfer*.

Were there famous surfers before the magazines? Fewer than a handful: Duke Kahanamoku, George Freeth, and Tom Blake were probably the only wave-riders any nonsurfer had heard of during the first five decades of the twentieth century— and were truly famous. But were there surfers of renown, recognized up and down the coast for their superior skill? Certainly. From the nascent surf-movie scene of the 1950s emerged the sport's first cult of personality, as filmmakers like Bud Browne, John Severson, Greg Noll, and Bruce Brown cast their 16 mm montages with the top performers of the day. The throngs of hooting surfers who packed the Vets halls and high school auditoriums were cheering at the first modern representation of themselves— but an idealized version, more talented on the board. Yet aside from the comedy sequences in

which the surfers generally (and good naturedly) made fools of themselves, the early surf flicks portrayed little more than that talent; you didn't learn anything about the surfers beyond the drop-knee turns and slapstick.

This, then, was SURFER's first major cultural contribution, providing a regular forum for the bimonthly examination of surfing's top personalities and at the same time shaping our collective vision of ourselves.

It all started in 1963 with the Surfer Poll, in which readers voted for their favorite surfers. Before the poll, the magazine's content often had a high-school-yearbook feel, with "Surfer By Day, Maître d' By Night"–type features. The Surfer Poll changed all that by introducing the concept of surf stardom and quantifying it. Readers earnestly scratched their heroes' names on a provided ballot page, folded it carefully into an envelope, then licked, stamped, and mailed it—total involvement. That seminal 1963 poll, won by Phil Edwards, featured the most diverse collection of personalities ever tallied: characters like Greg Noll, Rick Grigg, John Peck, Mickey Muñoz, Midget Farrelly, and Dewey Weber. Today's polls—of both men and women—have narrowed the spectrum somewhat, emphasizing professional competitive success as much as sheer exposure. (Laird Hamilton has never placed on the Surfer Poll, nor have multiple longboard world-title winners or style icons Joel Tudor and Daize Shayne.) That's not to say that passion doesn't play a role in the voting: There have been only three men's winners in the past twenty years. It's obvious that Californian Tom Curren and Floridian Kelly Slater (who has won the poll a staggering fifteen times) have captured the imaginations of SURFER readers in a manner that transcends mere pro rankings.

The enigmatic Mickey Dora appeared on the Surfer Poll only once, placing fourth in 1965, yet he remains, even after his death in 2002, the most fascinating surf personality ever. Strangely enough, this is primarily due to his relationship with SURFER, which over the decades functioned as the main source of information about him. In a series of surly interviews, subversive advertisements, elaborate hoaxes, disingenuous essays, and classic diatribes that spanned three decades, Dora used SURFER's pages as his pulpit, carefully constructing an enduring mystique. Virtually everything the surfing world knew, or thought it knew, about Dora was gleaned from his sporadic appearances in the magazine he claimed to detest—and, in fact, blamed for most of surfing's ills.

Maybe a SURFER profile would've shed light onto some of Dora's dark places. Throughout the 1960s and well into the '70s the SURFER interview was the main platform for celebrity. Then

in the mid-'70s a series of in-depth personality profiles began appearing, penned by Australian journalists Phil Jarrett and John Witzig. Jarrett, especially, brought unprecedented journalistic sensibility to the surf milieu (honed, no doubt, during his stint at Australian *Playboy*), providing not only a portrait but also the writer's perspective in features like "Shaun at the Crossroads" (October 1978) and "Still Reno After All These Years" (April 1979).

"There is no doubt in his mind that he is sitting on a royal flush," wrote Jarrett in his '78 profile of South African superstar Shaun Tomson. "His self-assurance is almost frightening, but there are times when you can sense his vulnerability . . . times when you catch glimpses of the spoiled rich kid or the Jewish family boy who would rather not go home than to go home a failure."

Since then, the SURFER profile has endeavored to present three-dimensional surf stars, with the best pieces dealing with both high and low points—Kimball Taylor's 2009 profile of Darryl "Flea" Virostko being a perfect example. Flea's

harrowing depiction of alcohol and methamphetamine addiction—including the admission that he and many other famous Santa Cruz big-wave riders rode giant Mavericks while on meth—infused contemporary surf stardom with a cold dose of reality and earned respect for Virostko's candor mixed with outrage at what has turned out to be a false ideal.

We would not be without our Fleas, however. Or our Phils, our Doras, our Corkys, Davids, Joyces, Nats, Owls, Margos, Lopezes (Gerry, Shea, and Cory). Or our Rabbits, PTs, MRs, TCs, and CJs. Or Andy, Bruce, Kelly, Jordy, Dane. Or Lisa, Layne, Carissa, and Coco. Or any of the other characters who have populated the pages of SURFER during the past fifty years, each and every one of them helping to define not only a lifestyle, but also a style of life. —SG

POWER ISSUE COVER AND OUTTAKE: (L–R) **ANDY IRONS**, **LAIRD HAMILTON**, **KELLY SLATER**, **CHRISTIANA JANNSEN**, **JOEL TUDOR**, **LILA METZGER**, **RANDY HILD**, **TAYLOR STEELE**, **FERNANDO AGUIRR**, AND **BRUCE IRONS**.

preceding spread: IN 2003 **MICK FANNING'S** SIGNATURE SANDAL CAME WITH A BUILT-IN BOTTLE OPENER, WHICH EXPLAINS THIS MOMENT OF SURFER POLL MAYHEM WITH FOURTEEN-TIME WINNER **KELLY SLATER**.

1 STYLISH **BILLY HAMILTON** WITH STYLIST MINI-GUN, CIRCA 1968. **2** **CHEYNE HORAN,** THE GREATEST, MOST POPULAR SURFER NEVER TO WIN A WORLD TITLE OR A SURFER POLL. **3** INSIGHTFUL SURFER/AUTEUR **CHRIS MALLOY.** **4** HAWAIIAN ICON **MICHAEL HO,** MENEHUNE NO LONGER. **5** THE ENIGMATIC **TOM CURREN,** WHOSE LEGEND LITERALLY GREW UP IN THE PAGES OF *SURFER.* **6** THE IRREPRESSIBLE MONTGOMERY "BUTTONS" KALUHIOKALANI. **7** MID-'70S FRIENDS AND RIVALS **MICHAEL TOMSON, MARK RICHARDS,** AND **RORY RUSSELL** **8** THE TWO MAIN FACES OF 1960S WOMEN'S SURFING: **MARGO GODFREY** (LEFT) AND **JOYCE HOFFMAN.**

"I JUST WANT TO FALL IN LOVE WITH THE SPORT THAT GAVE ME EVERYTHING."

ANDY IRONS

FROM "THE WEIRD YEAR," MARCH 2009

opposite: ANDY IRONS, NOT ENTIRELY BUSTED UP ABOUT HIS BUSTED STICK.

THE ART OF RISK

BY STEVE HAWK

STEVE HAWK

WHEN I THINK ABOUT THE FEW ARTICLES I EDITED THAT INVOLVED TRUE RISK—THE KIND THAT COMES WITH THE CHANCE OF A PERSON COMING HOME IN A BODY BAG—I INEVITABLY THINK BACK TO THE STECYK-BREWER DEBACLE IN JAVA.

The 38-foot fax arrived in the night, a gripping handwritten account of an Indo surf excursion disrupted by storms, snakes, gun smugglers, disabled boats, food shortages, and a near-fatal reef-bounce. This was the early '90s—before e-mail and Twitter and throwaway cell phones— and like all previous editors of SURFER, we'd grown accustomed to writers delivering their stories in weird ways—journals scrawled on airliner barf bags, unlabeled cassette tapes of aimless interviews, and many last-minute faxes from ASP correspondent Derek Hynd.

But this was something altogether new: a fax the length of four longboards curled up on the floor when we arrived for work one day. Writer Craig Stecyk, using the nom de plume John Smythe, had penned a long, yet oddly cryptic series of vignettes titled "The Annals of Disaster." It was about a disastrous boat trip he'd taken to Java with photographer Art Brewer and several pro surfers, one of whom ended up

DANGER WAVE SURFING HAS BEEN TAKEN TO A WHOLE NEW LEVEL BY NEW MILLENNIUM HELLMEN LIKE **GREG LONG** (PICTURED HERE AT AN UNNAMED BREAK IN BAJA) WHO, ARMED WITH JET-SKIS, WEATHER MAPS, AND AN APPARENT LACK OF ANYTHING RESEMBLING FEAR, ARE CHARGING WAVES THAT PREVIOUS GENERATIONS SHRUNK FROM.

getting evacuated to a Singapore hospital. Ever the eccentric, Stecyk scribbled his erudite tome on a roll of butcher paper and faxed it over as a single page. It seemed we had no choice but to unfurl it on the floor and measure its length, which of course only heightened my guilt when I handed the scroll to an assistant editor tasked with typing it up.

It was worth the headache: Stecyk's piece is one of the most harrowing surf-travel stories ever published. Not long into the journey, after dispatching their boat to fetch medical help for the injured Tim Heyland, the crew found itself stranded on an island off western Java for four days. "Living on coconuts and fish, with absolutely no way to medicate Heyland, some of us begin to lose faith," Stecyk wrote. "We are stuck on an unpopulated, uncharted, remote island with meager alternatives. And to add to the tension, we have been forced to watch three days of solid, ten-foot, open-ocean bumps march

toward the next group of islands, a painful indication that the surf is going off elsewhere."

The point I want to make here is that the strange paths by which words arrive at SURFER was (and still is) ultimately irrelevant—as long as the stories have heart and the editors have time and talent enough to massage them, design them, and get them to the printer before the presses roll. Our subculture's heritage remains enriched because so many of its adventurers tell good tales and because, for half a century now, we've been blessed with a custom-shaped medium adept at sharing those tales with the flock.

And so when I look back at the hundred or so issues of SURFER in which my name sits atop the masthead, from April 1991 to May 1999, I'm proudest of the pages in which we managed to arrange a potent pairing of writer and subject. When it works—when an assignment meshes with a particular writer's temperament,

perceptiveness, and style—the result is greater than the sum of its parts. It's art.

The '90s was a good time to be running a surf mag. The decade abounded in newsworthy moments and tectonic shifts: the unveiling of Mavericks and concurrent return of big-wave riding; the female uprising; the birth of tow-in; the comebacks of Tom Curren and Mark Occhilupo and their ultimate replacement by Kelly Slater and his fellow Momentum stars; the resurrection of longboarding; the discovery of cold-water gold in places like Alaska and Iceland.

My own luck extended to the dream team of writers orbiting within the magazine's gravitational field. SURFER in the '90s had access to nearly every great surf journalist on the planet, most of whom have gone on to do even greater things, writers like Tim Baker, Steve Barilotti, Jason Borte, Dan Duane, Matt George, Sam George, Derek Hynd, Bruce Jenkins,

Ben Marcus, Chris Mauro, Kem Nunn, Dave Parmenter, Derek Rielly, Evan Slater, Kimball Taylor, Matt Walker, and Matt Warshaw.

Of that cast, no one was better at turning an interview into art than Ben Marcus, my right-hand editor for many years and one of surf journalism's unsung talents. Ben's interviews with and profiles of Laird Hamilton, Sean Briley, Jeff Clark, Jay Moriarity, Lisa Andersen, Woody Brown, and others should be compiled into a book and distributed to students of the craft. He invariably drilled to the core and got people to reveal things they'd never before discussed in print. It helped that he was witty and smart, but his biggest gift was an ability to listen before asking his next question. Ben could also be a lunatic, and I was ultimately forced to fire him when he sucker-punched one of our ad guys.

Not surprisingly, the stories that tend to stand out in my mind involved risk. In 1994, Jenkins flew to Cabo San Lucas in search of Pat Curren, with no guarantee he'd even get an audience with the legendary recluse. In fact, Pat had sent word through friends that he didn't want to be interviewed. But Bruce persevered, showed up at Curren's beat-up trailer with a case of beer and a humble spirit, and persuaded him to talk about the early days at Waimea and about his famous son Tom, the world champ, whom he hadn't seen in years.

We sent Parmenter to Alaska with photographer Bob Barbour and surfers Brock Little and Josh Mulcoy on a wing and a rumor. It would have been a massively expensive skunk, and I started to fret openly when the crew went incommunicado for two weeks. It turns out the waves had

been green and alluring, and the article (January 1993) remains my favorite travel story ever to run in a surf mag.

When Mark Foo drowned in front of the cameras at Mavericks in December 1994, we were only days away from our monthly press run. Warshaw, my predecessor as SURFER's editor and now surfing's foremost historian, agreed to write not only the story of Foo's death but also a separate profile of his life. Two big centerpiece articles, on deadline. He pulled it off, and the issue, with sixteen-year-old Jay Moriarity's crucifixion wipeout on the cover (June 1995), never fails to move me when I page through it.

Similarly, we were two days from going to press in April 1996 when Slater vaulted past Sunny Garcia and Rob Machado to win the ASP world title in the final heat of the final contest of the year. This was the day of the famous Slater-Machado "high-five." Photographer Tom Servais raced straight from the beach to an airplane to a Southern California photo house that could develop his (predigital) slides on the spot. Barilotti and I stayed up all night in a North Shore rental writing and editing his piece. Joni Casimiro, our indefatigable art director, designed the article and revised the cover that morning and FedExed it to the printer that afternoon. We scooped the competition by a whole issue.

There was risk too in the decision to bring in guest editors to try to shorten the distance between readers and their heroes. If the real editors were worried about handing off the magazine to a couple of twenty-one-year-olds who barely knew how to type (Kelly Slater and Shane Dorian, October 1994), the polite young pros calmed us with their energy and aplomb. "I was a kid," Dorian said recently of his two-week stint at the magazine. "I didn't know enough to get nervous."

But those were abstract risks, risks of commerce and reputation. When I think about the few articles I edited that involved true risk—the kind that comes with the chance of a person coming home in a body bag—I inevitably think back to the Stecyk-Brewer debacle in Java.

I called Stecyk recently to see if he recalled writing and sending that thirteen-yard fax. Yes, he said, of course. He remembered it well. He remembered hanging it up on the side of a building and standing back to admire it as if it were a piece of art. But he didn't really want to talk about the fax. He got more excited talking about the trip itself.

"It was bleak," he said. "We were at the edge of a cyclone that killed more than one hundred thousand people in Bangladesh. There were bodies in the water. Our boat got wrecked when it hit a log. Everybody we ran into had automatic weapons. Just crazy, crazy fucked-up shit."

He went on that way for a while. I wish I had it on tape so I could share the whole thing with you.

THE ART OF BREWER

There have been SURFER photographers who specialize in action, those who specialize in scenics, and
those who specialize in portraits. Then there's Art
Brewer. Since first picking up a camera in the mid-
1960s, when as a Laguna Beach high schooler he got
his first job shooting the Hobie Team, Brewer has
adjusted his aperture through more significant surfing eras than any other photographer: SURFER cover
shots spanning five decades—any questions? But
for all the fantastic surfing the big man has shot,
the medium in which Brewer has left his most indelible mark is portraiture. SURFER has always been
rich in personality shots: If there's ever been a more
photogenic subculture than surfing, we haven't
seen it. Point a lens at any beach, and you're bound
to come up with a great character study. But the
formal portrait is a different animal entirely—and so
is Art Brewer. Irascible, demanding, often surly, by
his very demeanor Brewer commands respect. But
the brusqueness masks a genuine interest in his
subjects—a deeper affection, one might say—that
allows Brewer to take what is in fact a very deliberate composition and transform it into something
honest, almost spontaneous. A lot of that has to
do with his own prestige—to sit for an Art Brewer
portrait has always been one of surfing's real honors.
But what an Art Brewer portrait really boils down to
is trust, his subjects feeling safe under the eyes and
in the hands that have focused on so much of our
history. ▬

opposite: TOM STONE, 1969. ❶ NATHAN FLORENCE, 2001. ❷ LISA ANDERSEN, 1993.
❸ JOHNNY BOY GOMES, 1997.

IN DEEP

He was embedded long before they invented the word. And perhaps contributing editor/photographer Matt George would have been happier as a battle-field reporter, having once described his technique for covering a surf contest as ". . . the same way I would cover a civil war." But George is a photojournalist in the true sense of the word—no other reporter in SURFER history has shown his ability to both write about *and* photograph his subjects in such an inti-mate manner. And we mean intimate. When in Cocoa Beach writing the magazine's first profile on then teenage superstar-to-be Kelly Slater, George was surprised when Kelly's mom had him bunk down with Slater for the night instead of putting him on the couch. George wrote about what it was like to lie there listening to the future best surfer in the world sleep quietly before the tidal wave of expectation hit. SURFER editors found this a little *too* involved and edited the piece to have George standing at the bedroom door, watching Kelly's slumber—far creepier, considering the title, "The Seduction of Kelly Slater." But this sort of personal rapport led to a remarkable portrait of a pensive young star, very different from his characteristic "It's great to be me!" snapshots. ▬

❶ BETHANY HAMILTON, 2003. ❷ ROB MACHADO, 2001.
opposite: KELLY SLATER, 1989.

TOP **10** MALE SURFERS
WHOSE NAMES
SOUND LIKE PORN STARS

1. NICK WOOD
2. PETE ROCKY
3. LOVE HODEL
4. TAYLOR STEELE
5. DAMIEN HARDMAN
6. BONGA PERKINS
7. WINGNUT
8. BUZZY KERBOX
9. ALEX COX
10. SHANE STONEMAN

TOP **5** FEMALE SURFERS
WHOSE NAMES
SOUND LIKE PORN STARS

1. DAIZE SHAYNE
2. VERONICA KAY
3. GIDGET
4. KYLIE WEBB
5. KIM HAMROCK

FROM "SECTIONS," JULY 1998

POLL POSITION

On Saturday, April 25, 1964, ebullient master of ceremonies Brennan "Hevs" McClelland stood in front of a portable microphone set up on a table at the Bayou Restaurant in Dana Point calling for quiet.

"Tonight we're going to recognize these men according to a poll in which literally thousands of readers have responded," boomed McClelland. "When you see the twenty men who gather behind me on the speaker's platform you'll finally shake your head and you may change the order a little bit in your own minds, but you'll say, 'By golly, there are some fantastic surfers up there.'"

A lot has changed in regard to the annual Surfer Poll, including cutting the field down to ten and adding women for the 1964 Poll, dropping it completely during the antiestablishment early '70s, adding video awards in the mid-'90s, and eventually moving the entire extravaganza to Anaheim's sumptuous Grove Theater. But when it comes to summing up the essence of a popularity poll involving the best surfers in the world, nobody has ever said it better than did "Hevs" on that spring night at the Bayou. ▬

THEY LOOK LIKE WE DO

In the first half of the last century, the question "What does a surfer look like?" might have elicited a number of different descriptions, depending on where you asked. Most traveling folk would invoke the Hawaiian beachboy stereotype; Jack London's "bronzed Mercury." The earliest surf films offered yet another image to Californians: the tanned, muscular ex-serviceman look that most '50s wave riders exemplified. But with the advent of a regularly published magazine, surfers found a source of identification that bound together all various factions into a uniform archetype. By the 1970s, a surfer in Piha, New Zealand, looked pretty much like a surfer in, say, Houston, Texas. Consider Holly Rainey and Doug Swenson, respective winners of the 1972 Texas State Championships and both completely recognizable as faithful members of the tribe. ▬

❶ (BACK ROW) JOEY CABELL, GREG NOLL, RICK GRIGG, PHIL EDWARDS, PAUL STRAUCH, MIKE DOYLE, JOHN PECK, HOBIE ALTER (FRONT ROW) BUTCH VAN ARTSDALEN, CORKY CARROLL, MICKEY MUÑOZ, PAT CURREN, L. J. RICHARDS, DEWEY WEBER. ❷ THE STATE OF BEING A SURFER, CIRCA '72: YOU'D NEVER KNOW IF YOU DIDN'T LOOK CLOSELY AT THE TROPHIES.

THE SURFER PROFILE

MATT GEORGE

BY MATT GEORGE

THE ART OF DEVELOPING A PROFILE RELIES ON THE ABILITY TO NOT JUST HEAR WHAT THE SUBJECT IS SAYING, BUT ALSO TO LISTEN TO WHAT SHE OR HE IS *NOT* SAYING.

They are inside you, inside your dreams, indelible. And we need them to exist. Just as they need us to exist. And that is why SURFER has taken the task of writing profiles of our famous surfers seriously. And that is why, in my twenty-five-year tenure, I have insisted on not just calling on these surfers but also living with them; eating with them; traveling with them; surfing with them; and *knowing* them, their countries and families, and their hopes, ambitions, nightmares, and dreams.

I do this so that we may all know them.

And, in doing so, come to know ourselves.

BETWEEN THE LINES 1
BETHANY HAMILTON 2004

One month after the violent loss of her left arm, Bethany Hamilton and I were standing at Pine Trees on Kauai checking the surf. She stood there in her pretty flowered bikini, a couple of Band-Aids over the stump. A little local kid was staring at her Band-Aids, confused.

It was making me a little uncomfortable. Bethany didn't seem to notice.

"Hey . . . where's your arm?" the kid finally asked.

Bethany looked at him and replied easily, "A tiger shark bit it off a month ago."

A few moments passed. Then the kid shrugged, and the both of them looked back out over the surf.

The kid said, "So, where we gonna paddle out?"

Bethany raised her right arm and pointed to what looked like a small workable left.

"Right there," she said.

I had tears in my eyes at the monumental courage of this thirteen-year-old girl. I couldn't help it.

Not just to scratch the surface, but to actually get to *know* these heroes of ours is essential to the way each of us understands our own surfing identity. Like it or not, these famous surfers influence the way we dress, the way we think, the way we see ourselves, the way we see others, what we ride, what we value, what we believe, what we do, the way we surf, the way we speak—the very way we live and love.

And man, if that's not one of the most important truths for any surfer to accept, I don't know what is.

This is the essence of the Surfer Profile.

Seeking the hero's humanness.

Reveal this, and we reveal our own.

BETWEEN THE LINES 2
CHEYNE HORAN 1988

I stood there on the sidewalk of the main street of Byron Bay, Australia, staring at a stranger reflected in the picture window of a grocery store.

The stranger was me.

I had just spent a week up-country on Cheyne Horan's alternative-lifestyle commune—vegetarian dogs, yoga, starfins, cries of passion in the night down the hall, and constant "herbal enchantment." The stranger in the reflection in the picture window was unshaved for days, with bloodshot eyes and matted hair. He was shirtless and carried a plastic bag of garden carrots under his arm. Leaves and grass were melted into the wax of his board.

God only knows where he got the ratty hippie bag slung over his shoulder . . . or what was in it.

And all I could do was just stand there looking at myself in that picture window, wondering when I had stopped wearing shoes.

Immersion is the foundation of true profiling. Our outlook is transformed by stepping into the hero's world. We emerge with new understanding of both him and ourselves.

BETWEEN THE LINES 3
THE FREE RIDE BOYS 2008

I had previously written about each one of the four, and now I would see them honored together.

An aura of muscular power emanated from the table where they sat together at the 2008 Surfer Poll awards: Shaun Tomson, Rabbit Bartholomew, Ian Cairns, Peter Townend. Older, grayer, bowed by time, but with shoulders still as strong as oxen, they sat awaiting the award for their documentary Bustin' Down the Door. *I caught Rabbit's eyes; he winked and mimed, tipping an imaginary hat, an old custom of ours since we*

first worked together back in '86. I tipped mine back. Then I looked at Shaun. He smiled that ear-to-ear grin, all teeth, and started softly laughing; we've always gotten a kick out of each other over the years, reminding ourselves how lucky and outrageous we were to be surfers. Big Ian, eyes a little rheumy and haunted, but still impressive with that unshakable confidence, gave me a simple nod. And Peter, forever Pan, gave me both thumbs. He was stoked to be here, so stoked to be a piece of our history. As the tribute introduction began, each of them straightened a little, getting ready for the applause they had heard many times before, eyes calm but riveted on the stage—a stage they had taken many times before. Just before they stood, Rabbit reached over and patted Shaun on the back. I was just close enough to catch what he said. "We did it, mate." Then the place erupted with applause, and the spotlight found them, and they stood to make their way to the podium.

These men were proud.

And so, may the saints preserve us all, were we.

Without the Surfer Profile, these people would never have been kings.

So many of our lives are defined by the era when our kings and queens of choice reigned.

Without the profile, we would never have known the madness of Cheyne Horan; the private troubled world of Tom Curren; the savant child inside Mark Occhilupo; the inner power of Keala Kennelly, a woman alone; or the extraordinary will of Layne Beachley or of her real name, Tanya Maris. We would never have known the suicide hauntings of Oscar Wright or the heartache of the beautiful Beau Young. The story I wrote about Beau's troubled relationship with his famous father, Nat, caused such Aussie outrage that a Sydney Herald headline splashed: "Seppo journo bashes Nat!"

Yet there was one that got away, one I never wrote about. There was a reason I did not write this particular Surfer Profile, but in the spirit of my responsibility to the magazine, I will share a passage from my notes with you now.

BETWEEN THE LINES 4
DAVE KALAMA 2004

NOTE: Dave Kalama and his children are so pure, so connected to the Hawaiian islands and their ocean life that, for the first time in my life, I feel like an intruder. Dave has perfected a synthesis between his Polynesian roots and surfing's NASA program with the rest of the Maui tow-in astronauts. Dave Kalama is an Olympian.

NOTE: Last night after dinner at Dave's island bungalow, his kids were tussling, playing, and shrieking in the living room as Dave and I sat down to record some words. Dave smiled, got up, popped a video in the TV, came back, and sat down ready to talk. There was suddenly absolute silence in the living room. Curious, I walked over to check it out. His kids were looking at the TV screen, rapt. The little boy was standing, his head cocked curiously to the right. On screen was ethereal footage of dolphins at play in the sea, perfect aquatic forms flowing in concert with the ocean. The tape had been a gift from a friend of Dave's—his latest footage shot from extraordinary angles. The kids swayed to the movements of the waves and the animals before them, as natural as heartbeats. I was stunned. Dave just smiled at me.

"They see things most people don't," he said.

I didn't know whether he was talking about his kids or the dolphins.

NOTE: Eleven hours later, and here I am on a plane taking off for a new assignment. I am climbing out of Maui, flying directly over a surf spot called Speckles, private training ground for the tow-in elite. I look out the window and can see looping circles of wake as the tow-in crew whips themselves into wave after wave. I know Dave is down there. Living simply. Perfectly. Synchronized between heaven and Earth.

Then clouds obscure my view.

NOTE: Sitting back in my seat, I realize that I am not going to write a profile on Dave Kalama. For the first time in my life, I do not want to do a damn thing that might cause so much as a ripple in such a glassy spiritual pond. I do not regret it.

No one needs to know Dave Kalama's secrets. There aren't any.

He sits upon Mt. Olympus.

No one needs to hear that from me.

The Surfer Profile has both preserved history and showcased the future. And my twenty-five-year running commentary on my friend Kelly Slater, our longest-reigning king, have done both. Kelly has been the future since I first wrote about him at fifteen. Now, at thirty-seven, he is finally of the age to question the very future whose course he has almost singlehandedly set.

And, as is the way of our world, the Surfer Profile was there:

following spread: WITH THE BOOST MOBILE PRO AT LOWER TRESTLES DROPPING THE ASP WORLD CHAMPIONSHIP TOUR INTO *SURFER'S* BACKYARD, THE MAG'S COVERAGE OF COMPETITIVE SURFING GOT EVEN MORE INTIMATE. TAJ BURROW, SIGNING OFF ON SOCAL SURF FANS.

PAGE

64

BETWEEN THE LINES 5
KELLY SLATER 2009

Those moss green eyes were looking into mine again, and I must say it was damned good to see how bright they still burned after all these years.

I had never seen Kelly Slater so fit. He looked in better shape than the eighteen-year-olds in the room.

He and I sat together and chatted in the soft heat of a Bali night. We were at Rizal Tanjung's balcony restaurant waiting for the lights to go down. It seemed the whole world was there—all the heroes. The Rip Curl contest had ended earlier that day, and we had all gathered for a first look at Taylor Steele's new movie, Stranger than Fiction. Kelly had his pretty girlfriend in hand, and he softly stroked her forearm, gingerly sipping his red wine as we caught up on life's great events. The party swirled around us, but Kelly was in a thoughtful mood. I'd seen him like this before. He had something to say but wasn't quite sure when to say it.

When the lights went down and the movie started, Kelly leaned forward in the darkness, his elbows on his knees and his hands clasped. He watched intently. His face at my shoulder, he began asking all sorts of questions about the surfing on the screen. I whispered my answers. He was very quiet about it, didn't want to broadcast anything. He would comment simply from time to time as the best surfing the planet had to offer sailed across the screen above the packed, boozy bar.

Kelly: No power, not enough rocker, can't read waves, needs a better shaper, doesn't know where the power is, no bottom turn, too much time in the air, should look down the line more, too much time in beachbreaks. Board's too small. Hawaii will kill him. Doesn't understand accelerating in the tube . . .

There was no ego in what Kelly was saying, no bitterness or sour grapes, just experienced, honest, pinpoint accurate observation.

Eventually the lights came up and the party began to howl. Dean Morrison and the Aussies already had the proverbial lampshades on their heads. But Kelly remained quiet amidst the madness. Most could feel it and were giving him plenty of room. He hesitated a moment, looked around the room, leveled his eyes on me, and then finally said what was on his mind:

Kelly, with genuine concern: "Who's gonna take my place? I can't do this forever. Competitively . . . who is gonna take my place?"

We looked around together.

Bruce Irons had just won the contest, but we all knew he was going to quit the tour any second.

Brother Andy was over in the corner surrounded by fans, looking fragile, trying real hard not to drink or accept any of the proffered drugs, looking like there was nothing to worry about . . . except for everything in the whole goddamned world.

The rest of the young guns in the room were incoherent, intoxicated with the free booze and the free weight of their own too-early, unearned fame and riches.

I looked back at Kelly, and he just smiled that lonely smile of his. Then he squeezed my shoulder and stood, and made his way out of the place with his girlfriend and a quiet dignity.

I watched him go.

And I was damned if I knew the answer to his question.

Surfing is on all of our minds, in all of our hearts.

And though our heroes fight it out in the arena, the Surfer Profile leads the way, making sure our sport's pantheon lives forever in these pages.

And so they should.

They are who you are.

And if you are passionate enough and you read closely enough . . . you too will live forever in these pages.

Q: WHAT DOES BEING A PRO SURFER MEAN TO YOU?

"WELL, IT'S MORE THAN SURFING. IT'S PERSONALITY, AS WELL. AND IT'S WEIRD FOR ME TO SAY THIS, BUT LOOKS ARE IMPORTANT. LOOKS MAKE A BIG DIFFERENCE. A LOT OF PEOPLE AREN'T GOING TO UNDERSTAND THIS, OR THEY'RE GOING TO THINK I'M AN IDIOT, BUT THAT'S THE WAY IT IS."

BRAD GERLACH
FROM "TALK SHOW," AUGUST 1987

TOP 10 MOST COMPELLING CHARACTERS

1. MICKEY DORA. NO OTHER SURFER EVEN COMES CLOSE. YET OUR DECADES-LONG FASCINATION WITH THE BLACK KNIGHT OF MALIBU ACTUALLY REVEALS A LOT MORE ABOUT US THAN IT DOES ABOUT MIKLOS SANDOR DORA. *THAT* MICKEY DORA WAS SIMPLY A MOODY, LONELY KID IN SEARCH OF A FATHER FIGURE WHO ALSO HAPPENED TO SURF WELL. *OUR* DORA, ON THE OTHER HAND, WAS THE ORIGINAL SURFING REBEL WHO TILTED AGAINST THE ESTABLISHMENT EVEN BEFORE THERE WAS AN ESTAB-LISHMENT, EMBODYING THE "F---K YOU" SPIRIT THAT VIRTUALLY EVERY SURFER FEELS AS HE OR SHE IS HEADED TOWARD THE BEACH WHILE EVERYONE ELSE IS GOING TO WORK. THAT MICKEY DORA CHOSE *SURFER* AS HIS PRIMARY PULPIT OVER THE YEARS ENSURED THAT HIS SUBVERSIVE DIATRIBES BECAME DOGMA; EVEN IN DEATH, THE DORA MYTH IS ALIVE AND WELL. HE REMAINS THE MOST INTERESTING SURFER IN MODERN HISTORY.

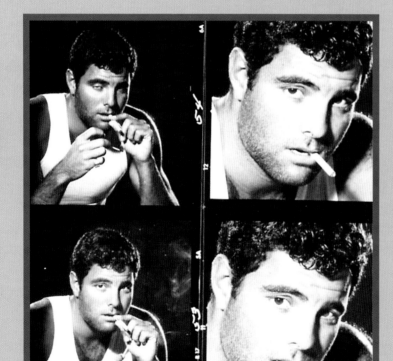

2. KELLY SLATER. FORGET ABOUT OMNIPOTENT POWER—WHAT MADE THE GODS ON MT. OLYMPUS SO APPEAL-ING WAS THEIR DECIDEDLY HUMAN ATTRIBUTES. SO WHILE ON HIS BOARD, KELLY CONTINUES TO THROW THUNDERBOLTS—THE SURFING HE DID TO WIN HIS RECORD NINTH WORLD TITLE WAS NOTHING IF NOT SUPERNATURAL—IT'S THE VERY HUMAN SLATER WHO HAS ENDEARED HIMSELF TO THREE GENERATIONS OF FELLOW SURFERS. BECAUSE DESPITE HIS PHENOMENAL TALENT, KELLY ALWAYS SEEMED LIKE A FELLOW SURFER—NO MYSTIQUE WHATSOEVER. HIS FAMILY ISSUES, HIS GIRLFRIEND PROBLEMS, HIS BALDING—WHEN IT COMES TO SELF-EXPRESSION, SLATER'S HEART HAS PERMA-NENTLY RESTED ON HIS SLEEVE. FROM HIS FIRST *SURFER* PROFILE MORE THAN TWENTY YEARS AGO TO HIS LATEST APPEARANCE DISCUSSING RECENT SURFBOARD INNO-VATIONS (WHEN WAS THE LAST TIME A TOP PRO SURFER DID THAT?), KELLY HAS GIVEN OF HIMSELF. LUCKY US.

3. GERRY LOPEZ. HE IS ARGUABLY THE GREATEST SURF STAR THE SPORT HAS EVER KNOWN, HAVING ACHIEVED ICONIC STATUS THE HARD WAY: WITHOUT MONTHLY MULTI-MILLION-DOLLAR MARKETING CAMPAIGNS, SPONSORED MENTAWAI BOAT TRIPS, AND DVDS. NO, GERRY LOPEZ BECAME THE MOST RECOGNIZABLE SURFER ON EARTH IN THE PRIMITIVE, BIMONTHLY *SURFER* ERA; *FIVE SUMMER STORIES* WOULD ROLL THROUGH TOWN ONCE A YEAR. YET SOMETHING IN THE WAY HE MOVED—THE ABSOLUTE APLOMB WITH WHICH HE RODE PIPE-LINE—APPEALED TO THE STYLIST IN ALL OF US. IT DIDN'T MATTER THAT WE TRIED TO SURF SECOND LIGHT IN COCOA BEACH THE WAY LOPEZ SURFED SECOND REEF PIPE. IT WAS STYLE, MAN, STYLE! THE BOWL CUT, THE MILIUS MOVIES, THE SPEEDOS AT G-LAND—WE WOULD FORGIVE LOPEZ ANYTHING FOR THE PRIVILEGE OF WATCH-ING HIM SURF.

4. TOM CURREN. THE LESS HE SAID, THE HAPPIER THE SURFING WORLD SEEMED TO BE WITH THE MESSAGE. HOT YOUNG SURFERS HAD GRACED THE PAGES OF *SURFER* BEFORE: JEFF HAKMAN, WAYNE LYNCH, ROLF AURNESS, CHRIS O'ROURKE, CHEYNE HORAN. BUT WHEN THE ELDEST SON OF LEGENDARY BIG-WAVE RIDER PAT CURREN QUIETLY, ALMOST CASUALLY MADE HIS WAY ONTO THE SCENE, SURF FANS BREATHED A COLLECTIVE SIGH OF RELIEF. FOLLOWING A NEW WAVE OF PRO SURFERS WHO SEEMINGLY HAD TO TRUMPET THEIR ACCOMPLISHMENTS, HERE WAS A PRODIGY WHO LET HIS PRETERNATURAL SKILL AND SYMBIOTIC RELATIONSHIP WITH THE OCEAN DO THE TALKING. FOR MORE THAN TWENTY-FIVE YEARS, WE'VE LIKED WHAT WE'VE HEARD.

5. NAT YOUNG. THERE CAN BE ONLY ONE, AND YET EVEN A QUICK SCAN OF *SURFER* BACK ISSUES REVEALS VERY FEW ERAS HAVE BOASTED AN UNDISPUTED "BEST." (HINT: WE'RE IN ONE RIGHT NOW. SEE NUMBER TWO ON THIS LIST.) PHIL EDWARDS HAD MIKE DOYLE TO CONTEND WITH; CURREN RAN NECK-IN-NECK WITH TITANS LIKE TOM CARROLL AND MARK OCCHILUPO. BUT FOR A FEW YEARS BETWEEN, SAY, 1966 AND 1969, ONE SURFER TOWERED OVER THE REST. AND IT WASN'T JUST THE MULTIPLE *SURFER* COVERS (FIVE, MORE THAN ANY OTHER SURFER IN THE 1960s) THAT MADE IT CLEAR THAT AUSTRALIA'S NAT YOUNG WAS "TOPS NOW." THERE HAD NEVER BEEN A SURFER MORE DOMINANT IN TERMS OF INNOVATION, COMPETITION, AND ATTITUDE. NOR HAS THERE BEEN SINCE.

6. DAVID NUUHIWA. CALL HIM KING OF THE CLOSEOUT. IN FACT DAVID NUUHIWA, LAUDED THROUGHOUT THE DECADES WITH *SURFER* COVERS AND POLL WINS, POPULAR SURFBOARD MODELS, AND FAN CLUBS, SURFED DAMN WELL IN MEDIUM-SIZE PIPELINE. BUT UNLIKE SO MANY OF HIS PEERS, DAVID (FIRST NAME ONLY, PLEASE) DIDN'T NEED TO PROVE ANYTHING AT SPOTS LIKE SUNSET BEACH OR WAIMEA. HE SURFED SO FLUIDLY, SO GRACEFULLY, SO ARTISTICALLY IN 2-FOOT 22ND STREET. HERMOSA OR JUNKY SOUTHSIDE H.B. PIER THAT HIS PERFORMANCES TRANSCENDED THE MEDIUM. HIS NOSE-RIDING: SUBLIME. HIS LATE '60S ROCK-STAR POSTURING ADDED LUSTER; HE WAS FUN TO WATCH. BUT BY TRANSFORMING AVERAGE SURF INTO SOMETHING WONDERFUL, DAVID NUUHIWA VALIDATED THE WONDERFULLY AVERAGE SURFER. THANK HIM EVERY DAY.

following spread: WITH ALL THE ELEMENTS OF SEVENTIES SURF STARDOM IN PLACE—THE SHADES, THE 'STACHE, THE LIGHTNING BOLT SWALLOWTAIL—**GERRY LOPEZ** DOMINATED THE PARKING LOT AT ALA MOANA, AND THE PAGES OF *SURFER*, LIKE NO CELEBRITY BEFORE OR SINCE.

7. LAIRD HAMILTON. HE'S BIGGER THAN HE LOOKS—AND HE LOOKS BIG. DURING THE PAST TWENTY-FIVE YEARS, LAIRD HAMILTON HAS COMPLETELY REDEFINED THE CONCEPT OF BIG. THAT'S RIGHT, IT'S BEEN MORE THAN TWO DECADES SINCE HIS LAIRDNESS FIRST APPEARED IN *SURFER*—HE HAD A COVER IN 1983. SINCE THEN, SURFING'S HERCULES (COMPLETE WITH HIS LABORS, 60-FOOT PEAHI STANDING IN FOR THE NEMEAN LION, UNTHINKABLE TEAHUPOO FOR THE DEADLY HYDRA) WENT ON TO BECOME THE MOST INFLUENTIAL, INNOVATIVE SURFER OF THE HALF CENTURY, INVENTING NOT ONLY NEW WAYS TO SURF—STRAPPED IN AND JET ASSISTED—BUT AN ENTIRELY NEW WAY OF LOOKING AT THE WORLD: HIS "OH MY GOD!" SURFER COVER USHERED IN THE ERA OF "THE SLAB."

8. LISA ANDERSEN. WHO KNEW THAT SURFING LIKE A GIRL MEANT SURFING LIKE A GUY? THERE WERE GREAT FEMALE CHAMPIONS BEFORE HER: JOYCE, MARGO, JERICHO, FRIEDA, JODIE, AND WENDY. FINE SURFERS, ALL. FINE CHAMPIONS. YET IT TOOK A TOMBOY FROM FLORIDA TO REALLY BREAK THROUGH THE FIBERGLASS CURTAIN. PUT PLAINLY, LISA WAS THE SPORT'S FIRST FEMALE CHAMPION WITHOUT "FOR A GIRL" TRAILING IN HER WAKE. SHE WAS JUST PLAIN HOT—THAT SHE GOT FED UP WITH WOMEN'S SWIMWEAR AND STARTED WEARING TRUNKS ONLY EMPHASIZED THIS FACT. WITH THAT SINGLE, LIBERATING STATEMENT, LISA INTRODUCED A WHOLE NEW BEING, A THIRD GENDER: GUYS, GIRLS, AND NOW ROXY GIRL. IN LIGHT OF THIS HITCH IN SURFING EVOLUTION, HER COMPETITIVE RECORD PALES: SHE'LL BE CONSIDERED THE GREATEST FOR A LONG TIME TO COME.

9. RABBIT BARTHOLOMEW. HE MAY NOT HAVE BEEN THE BEST, BUT HE WAS BEST AT PLAYING THE BEST. WAYNE "RABBIT" BARTHOLOMEW, DESPITE GROWING UP ON QUEENSLAND'S SURF-BLESSED GOLD COAST, WASN'T DEALT THE BEST HAND. MICHAEL PETERSON HAD FAR MORE TALENT, PT BETTER PRESS. SHAUN WAS DURBAN ROYALTY, MR'S DAD RAN A SURF SHOP, AND CHEYNE HORAN *LOOKED* MORE LIKE A PRO SURFER THAN DID THE SCRUFFY RABBIT. BUT NO ONE HAD MORE AMBITION, FIERCER DRIVE, OR A GRANDER VISION OF WHAT COULD BE THAN WAYNE BARTHOLOMEW. AND HE LAID HIMSELF ON THE LINE TO MAKE THAT VISION REALITY, IN THE WATER AND OUT. YOU COULD SAY TODAY'S PRO TOUR WOULD NOT BE WHAT IT IS TODAY WITHOUT HIM AND YOU WOULD NOT BE FAR OFF. RABBIT ISN'T JUST A PROFESSIONAL SURFER, HE *IS* PROFESSIONAL SURFING.

10. RELL SUNN. LONG BEFORE THE ROXY GIRL THERE WAS RELL, THE QUEEN OF MAKAHA. NO SURFER EVER HAS GRACED THE PAGES OF *SURFER* QUITE LIKE THE LATE RELL KAPOLIOKA'EHUKAI SUNN. A PIONEERING WOMAN SURFER? CERTAINLY. AN EXTRAORDINARY ROLE MODEL, NOT JUST FOR HER COURAGEOUS FIFTEEN-YEAR BATTLE WITH BREAST CANCER BUT ALSO AS A TOTALLY WELL-ROUNDED, BROADLY SKILLED "WATERMAN": SURFER, PADDLER, LIFEGUARD, DIVER, WORLD TRAVELER? OF COURSE. BUT SUNN'S TRUE LEGACY IS MEASURED NOT BY HOW MANY WORDS ARE NECESSARY TO DESCRIBE IT, BUT BY HOW FEW. "THE HEART OF THE SEA." THAT WAS RELL.

WHAT WE RIDE:
SURFER ON DESIGN

THE SACRED CRAFT

ON DECEMBER 5, 2005, CLARK FOAM, THE WORLD'S leading manufacturer of polyurethane surfboard foam, suddenly shut down its factory and immediately discontinued production and delivery. The ensuing shock waves hit SURFER first—the Clark factory was located just three exits up Interstate 5 from the SURFER offices in Capistrano Beach. But even as the waves broke over SURFER, SURFER broke the story. At the helm was Chris Mauro, a former pro competitor and surfboard shaper with more than a thousand boards to his credit. Mauro had been the driving force behind the revamped "Design Forum," a SURFER staple that in the first few years of the new millennium had developed from a curiosity column to the only regularly appearing examination of surfboard innovation—design and construction. So when the news that Clark Foam had inexplicably closed its doors—with absolutely no advance warning, telling waiting surfboard builders, "Sorry, no more blanks"—Mauro knew that the biggest board story in the history of the magazine was going down on his watch.

"Blank Monday" (as it was later dubbed by SURFER stalwart Ben Marcus) represented more than just an inconvenience. After all, in the fifty years since he had helped perfect the polyurethane foam surfboard, Gordon "Grubby" Clark had established and fervently maintained an extremely profitable monopoly in the surfboard industry. As a member of the original "Dana Point Mafia," which included manufacturer Hobie Alter, surfwear pioneers Walter and Flippy Hoffman, publisher John Severson, and filmmaker Bruce Brown, Clark was a primary

architect of the modern surfing experience. Throughout his career he remained a passionate innovator. But the enigmatic former engineer was ruthless when it came to competition—Clark regarded any other foam manufacturer as an interloper. For those who even suggested examining alternative materials—like polystyrene, or Styrofoam—Clark reserved a jihadist's zeal. SURFER editor Sam George, a longtime proponent of alternative manufacturing techniques, was his frequent nemesis. Once when George was interviewing him for a story on a surfboard lamination glitch attributed to new foam formulas, Clark blithely informed George that he was closing up his factory and moving it across the border into Tijuana where the EPA couldn't touch him—almost daring the infidel polystyrene-propagandist to print the obvious fabrication.

From his position on the masthead, George had for years endorsed free thinking, providing editorial space to innovators like Phil Becker and Bill Stewart (progenitors of the modern longboard), John Bradbury, Greg Loehr, and Gary Linden (all pursuing the polystyrene alternative), and fellow Central Coast alum Dave Parmenter (the Howard Hughes of hybrid). The magazine later polarized the surf community by acknowledging the contributions of Surftech, a Santa Cruz–based surfboard company whose "offshore" production technique—a high-tech adaptation of the sailboard industry's epoxy-polystyrene composite construction, manufactured in Thailand—was viewed by many traditionalists as surfing's Great Satan, the specter of prefab popouts and

Walmart models. Strange that so many readers chose this moment in surf history to stick their heads in the sand, considering that SURFER had been endorsing a veritable cornucopia of surfboards—good and bad—for the previous four decades.

In the October 1967 issue, SURFER ran "Men and Their Models," an "advertorial" feature that presented top-team riders from all the major surfboard manufacturers, along with the specifications and performance characteristics of their various signature models. Since an "advertorial" by definition guarantees advertisers editorial coverage in return for ad placement, this cleverly designed feature was disingenuous. Disingenuous but forgivable, because the miniprofiles of boards like Bob Cooper's Morey-Pope "Blue Machine," Rich Chew's Harbour "Banana," and Bob Purvey's Con "Ugly" (just a few of the more colorfully named models) provided more information about more surfboards than had been published in the preceding six years of SURFER. More important, in the diversity of its content, it presented the idea that surfboard design was almost endless in its variation: that there was no such thing as a "standard" board.

No, if "Men and Their Models" is to be faulted, it should be for not coming out a year earlier. By the time it hit the newsstands, the first shots of the Shortboard Revolution had already died Down Under, with vee-bottom boys like Bob McTavish, Midget Farrelly, and Nat Young laps ahead on the fast track. In fact, the very next issue of SURFER featured contest coverage in

which Corky Carroll won the Santa Cruz 4-A championship at Steamer Lane riding an 8'4" "miniboard." Surprise?

Having for various reasons arrived late for the miniboard express (see page 97), SURFER made up for lost time with its first major endorsement: an extensive two-part series on the new shortboards, by soon-to-be-editor Drew Kampion. The accompanying cover shot of Nat Young enclosed within the template of his wide-backed, Greenough-finned vee-bottom emphasized the declaration of independence like no advertisement could and was the first of only three times a singular surfboard has been featured on a SURFER cover. The second came in 1981, when a Simon Anderson–designed, three-fin Thruster was top model (see page 96).

Between those cover dates, plenty of surfboard innovations did make it into the pages of SURFER, some relevant, some less so, but all representing an almost continual design push. In the May 1972 issue, SURFER ran a design story that highlighted four new trends: the swallowtail, the broad-based fin, the keel fin, and the split-tail fish. Okay, so three out of four isn't bad. Several issues later came SURFER's most audacious design gambit: a full-blown feature on a previously unheard-of, never-before-seen, totally out-of-left-field (well, Oxnard, which is pretty far out there sociologically) board called the Bonzer. The Bonzer story featured arresting portraits of the board's bizarre double concaves and side runners, and was ripe with hydrodynamic charts and esoteric terms like "Bernuli's principle of lateral pressure" and "venturi effect." The feature represented such a huge leap in consciousness compared to the rest of the editorial content that it appeared to have been dropped into place from some distant future, when all surfboards had three fins and were designed by computer. The accompanying cover blurb said it all: "Radical New Board Design."

Despite SURFER's coverage, the wider surfing world did not jump on Bonzers en masse as they did with the shortboard and, some years later, the Thruster. But the Bonzer, along with the winger, the Stinger, and the twin-fin—as well as all the other surfboard designs featured over the decades—illustrate SURFER's commitment to the ongoing process of building the perfect board.

Of course, building that board was trickier following Clark's bombshell in 2005. The entire industry was thrown into a commercial tailslide by a serious lack of raw materials. Yet soon new cores would be developed and new alternatives would arise, and SURFER covered all that too. From that first morning when Chris Mauro broke the Clark scandal on surfermag.com, touching off a tsunami of mainstream press coverage, the magazine was in the thick of it. The very next SURFER cover put things in the proper perspective with an evocative studio portrait of a pristine shaped blank (the third board to ever make the cover) adorned with a single blurb: "This Changes Everything."

It always has. —SG

1 THE POWER OF THREE: **BONZER BROS CLIFF COLLINGE, DUNCAN** AND **MALCOLM CAMPBELL.** **2** EARLY '70S SWIVEL FIN—NICE TRY. **3** THE ALAIA TREND: MODERN TURN ON ANCIENT BOARD. **CHRISTIAN WACH.** **4** A GROM'S DELIGHT: **KOLOHE'S ANDINO'S** QUIVER. **5** V-BOTTOM VS THE MINI-GUN, CIRCA 1967 **6** FREE YOUR MIND: THE **AUGA BOYS** FROM MAUI, COMPLETE WITH NIGHTSURFING HEADLAMPS, CIRCA 1973. **7** BK'S RED SUNSET ROCKET, ABOUT TO BE OFFERED FOR EXAMINATION TO **GERRY LOPEZ** AND **HERBIE FLETCHER** (SITTING). **8** **LAIRD HAMILTON'S** SUPREMELY INNOVATIVE FOIL BOARD OFFERS THE FIRST TRULY NEW SURFING EXPERIENCE SINCE THE KOA WOOD *OLO.* **9** THE SURFBOARD, PRE–FLOWER POWER, DEFINED IN THIS 1965 JACOBS AD.

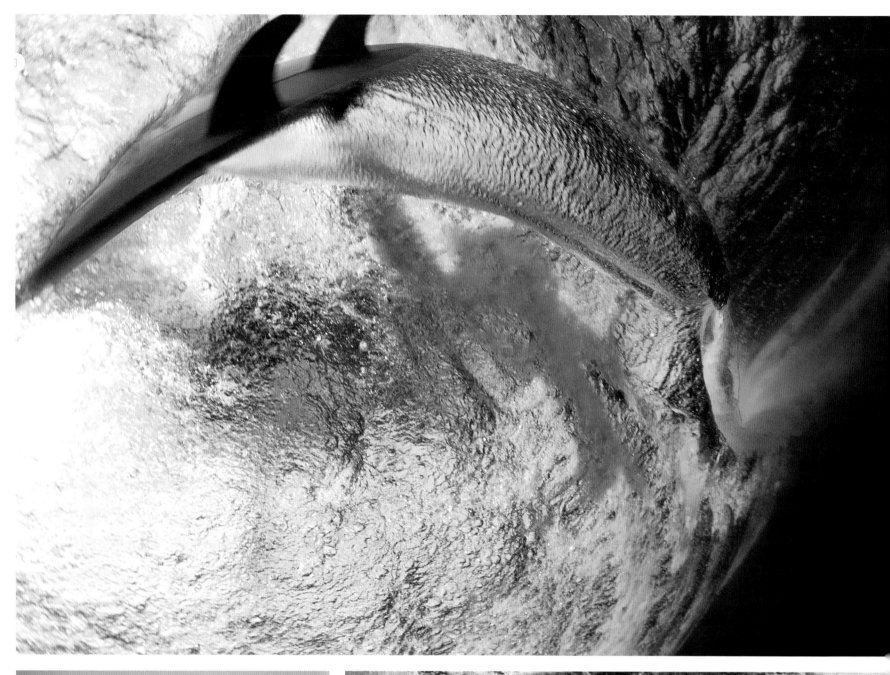

① MENTAWAI MASH-UP: **DAVE RASTOVICH** PUTS A STEVE LIS THROUGH ITS PACES. **②** TOM MOREY'S W.A.V.E. SET FIN ADS (FEATURING SKIP FRYE) SET THE STANDARD OF EXPERIMENTATION IN 1968. **③** SURFER STAFF PHOTOGRAPHER **TOM SERVAIS'** HYDRODYNAMICS STUDY. **④** OUT WITH THE OLD, IN WITH THE NEW: 1968 MINI-GUNS TAKE AIM AT SUNSET BEACH. **⑤** THE "SACRED CRAFT," A TERM COINED BY SURFERMAG.COM EDITOR SCOTT BASS, HAS ALWAYS BEEN A HANDS-ON EXPERIENCE. **GARY MOTIL**, 1979. **⑥** STICKER SHOCK: PIPE MASTER **JOEY BURAN'S** 1984 NORTH SHORE MYLAR FEST.

"WE TOOK BALSA AS FAR AS WE COULD, AND WHEN WE HIT THE WALL WE DEVELOPED POLYURETHANE FOAM. WHEN WE HIT THE WALL WITH POLYURETHANE FOAM, WE MOVED ON TO EPOXY-COMPOSITE. AND WHEN WE EVENTUALLY HIT THE WALL WITH THE COMPOSITES, WE'LL MOVE ON TO HOLLOW SHAPES. IT WON'T BE EASY AT FIRST—IT NEVER WAS. BUT WE'LL GET THERE."

REYNOLDS YATER
FROM "DESIGN FORUM: LIGHT IS RIGHT," APRIL 2004

opposite: **CHEYNE HORAN** CONFERS WITH AUSTRALIAN YACHT DESIGNER **BEN LEXAN** ON PERFORMANCE CHARACTERISTICS OF HIS "WINGED KEEL" FIN, CIRCA 1983. MANY CRITICS, INCLUDING MOST PERIOD *SURFER* EDITORS, FELT HORAN'S EXPERIMENTATION WITH BOTH THE FIN AND HIS BIZARRE MCCOY "LAZOR ZAP" SURFBOARD COST HIM SEVERAL WORLD TITLES.

EDITORIAL BY DESIGN

PAUL HOLMES

BY PAUL HOLMES

If it weren't true, it'd be almost funny, the way small events can have far-reaching effects. A butterfly flaps its wings in the jungles of Indonesia, and the East Coast gets hammered by a hurricane—that kind of thing. For me it was a plate of mussels eaten at the Hotel du Lac in Hossegor, France, in 1980.

Jim Kempton, soon to be promoted to publisher of SURFER, had just ordered another round of crusty bread to mop up the delicious juices in which the succulent shellfish had been cooked and served. And I'm sure we were well into the second bottle of wine. As we slurped and slobbered, he was telling me how he was having a terrible time finding a replacement for himself as editor at the magazine. He needed someone who was clued into pro surfing because it was clearly an emerging force, and he was concerned that rivals to "the bible of surfing" were getting ahead of the Good Book in covering it. Plus, he needed someone who knew surfboard design, because it was changing fast too.

As a former shaper and current editor of *Tracks* magazine in Sydney—where I was also contest director of the annual 2SM/Coca-Cola Surfabout, the world's most lucrative pro contest at the time—I didn't see that as a problem:

"I'll do it," I said.

"You would? You could? You will?"

"Sure," I said, on a whim, like a butterfly flapping its wings. "You organize the immigration stuff, and I'll be there."

Not only was it the best plate of *moules marinière* I'd ever had, it led to my overseeing one hundred issues of SURFER magazine, bringing several significant phases of surfboard evolution to popular attention, helping to advance the world pro tour, and spurring the quest to ride a 100-foot wave. Are you still with me? Let me explain.

SIMON ANDERSON WALKS THE WALK EN ROUTE TO HIS 1981 PIPELINE MASTERS VICTORY ON HIS
REVOLUTIONARY THREE-FIN "THRUSTER."

Kempton and I weren't in France simply to savor the local food and wine. The World Contest had just taken place, and both of us were there on assignment to see Australian Mark Scott win the men's title and Californian Alisa Schwartzstein the women's. But while both surfed well, it was the junior men's winner that had caught everyone's eye. From the first glance at Tom Curren, it was clear the sixteen-year-old Santa Barbaran had a bright future ahead of him. He had that inspired spark that suggested he could be a star, possibly the biggest of his generation—the surfer who might restore California surfing to its former place of glory. And he did, of course, once surfboard design caught up with what he was trying to do.

In the meantime, though, I returned to Australia and Kempton to the West Coast. It took more than twelve months to process my work visa. While I spent much of the time on tenterhooks at the mercy of the impenetrable INS bureaucracy, it was a hugely fascinating and productive year. Pending my arrival, Kempton had me work on a series of articles and profiles for SURFER about people and things going on Down Under—pretty much the undisputed power center of surfing at the time in board design, pro contests, surfwear labels, and more.

Among the articles I sent to Southern California was a piece on rising star Tom Carroll, who'd been the shop grommet at Col Smith and Wayne Warner's Morning Star Surfboards when I'd shaped there a couple or three years before. "Tommy Gun," as Col called him, was there nearly every afternoon after school to sweep up, run errands, or just hang out. Think AC/DC's Angus Young: tow-headed, tanned, and freckled, if not always in school uniform—rock 'n' roll transposed to surf culture—and you get the drift.

Everyone knew he was destined for fame.

Another in-depth piece I wrote during that year was about Simon Anderson, one of Carroll's heroes (seven years his senior). Anderson had won both the Bells and the Surfabout in 1977 and was rated number three in the world. But by the decade's end, he seemed stuck in the midranks of the top ten, and it was clear that surfers like him, who'd been at the forefront of pro surfing's launch, were coming under increasing pressure from a crop of younger rising stars like Carroll, Cheyne Horan, Dane Kealoha, Critta Byrne, Derek Hynd, Martin Potter, and Joey Buran, the sole Californian among the top sixteen.

Interestingly, Anderson, like many of the pro-tour pioneers—Michael Peterson, Terry Fitzgerald, Peter Townend, and Reno Abellira among them— were also surfboard shapers, making their own boards and adjusting their designs to the performance demands of the judging system and contest wave conditions. Ironically, one of the least experienced in the shaping room, Mark Richards, was by then the dominant force in pro surfing. He clinched his first world title in 1979, winning three of the thirteen events on the tour. The Wounded Gull rode his newly designed wing-swallow twin-fin. He backed it up with a repeat in 1980, when he won an incredible four of ten events, setting the stage for a record-breaking run of four world titles. That record wouldn't be beaten until Kelly Slater came on the scene more than a decade later. Richards's main competitor was Cheyne Horan, who rode a Geoff McCoy "no-nose" single-fin design: essentially a radical short "pig" with a superwide rolled-vee tail and wide point aft of center. Most of the top pro surfers at the time were riding single-fins, but there was a collective desire for change as they chased Richards's roster of results. Even the "King of the Round Pin Single-Fin" and 1978 World Champion Shaun Tomson switched to twin-fins in smaller surf conditions. Anderson was in a quandary. At 6'2" and 200 pounds, Richards excelled in medium and large surf, but as he explained to me in the interview for SURFER: "I was looking for something that would go good in small surf. I couldn't get that in a single-fin board. In an act of desperation, I went to twin-fins but then in bigger surf, when I needed it, I couldn't readjust to my single-fin . . . The obvious thing to do was to put a small single fin on the back of my twin-fin."

The creation that Anderson came up with—a narrow-nose wide squash tail winger board with three fins that he called the Thruster—turned out to be the ticket. If surfboard design has a destiny, then Anderson's original Thruster was its harbinger. In 1981 Anderson repeated history on the Aussie leg of the world pro tour, winning both at Bells Beach and the Surfabout. Bell's had been huge that year—12 to 15 feet—and the joke was that most of the touring pros, expecting smaller conditions and carrying twin-fins, had arrived with equipment that was "a foot too short and a fin too many." Anderson came with boards of the right length, and three fins proved to be just the right number.

Still, not everyone was convinced. Anderson, after all, was a formidable talent on any kind of equipment. Between two events, a skeptical Mark Richards told me that three-fin boards "are for people who can't ride twin-fins properly."

Hawaii was the ultimate proving ground, as always. When Anderson won the Pipeline Masters later that year, going left, backhand, and in double-overhead surf, there could be no doubt that a new era had begun.

In those days, the surf media paid little attention to surfboard design and how it related to results on the emergent world pro tour. That would change, and perhaps not be in the best interests of recreational surfers and weekend warriors who would as a result buy surfboards that were far too sophisticated—too small, too light, and too fragile—but were just like the pros were riding. SURFER's surfboard issue in mid-1981, produced shortly before my arrival at the magazine, addressed some of those issues even as

IN THE EARLY 1970S, BY THE TIME ISSUES OF *SURFER* HIT AUSTRALIA'S SHORES, THEY'D ALREADY BE SEVERAL MONTHS OLD. BUT AUSSIE SURFERS/ SHARPERS LIKE **PETER TOWNEND** LOST NO TIME COMING UP TO SPEED. HERE'S TOWNEND WITH HIS VERSION OF THE BONZER (AN AUSTRALIAN WORD FOR "BITCHIN") CIRCA 1973.

it digressed into a world of conjecture over designs like the asymmetric bi-fin and the flexible "Tinkler tail" and wandered into anachronism with a promotion of the tucked-under edge for rails—a concept that had been embraced by most shapers for almost a decade. Still, it did delve into multichannel-bottomed single-fins, which had found favor with some of the top pros.

Some would argue (I, for one) that those channels evolved into today's more subtle concave bottoms and double-barreled vees. But there was no mention at all of rocker or thickness distribution, both of which figured so heavily in the refinements that were to come. SURFER's editorial commentary was reserved in its assessment of the Thruster, saying that the new design was "beginning to make waves" and that "in an age of sophisticated twins and channel bottoms" the Thruster was being welcomed "in a true spirit of openmindedness." That was definitely the case among most of the top pros, Tom Carroll among the first, who quickly adopted the design. Even so, twin-fins had become so pervasive in the U.S. market by then that Gary

McNabb, owner of Nectar Surfboards and an early proponent of the Thruster, was quoted as saying, "A lot of kids can't surf these days. They just slide around . . . the Thruster is meant to go forward, not sideways."

Within the space of just a few months, the Thruster became standard issue on the pro tour—and it remains so to this day—although Richards never gave up on the twin-fin that served him so well.

So what were the selling points for the Thruster, aside from Anderson's results? The self-described power surfer summed it up nicely: "The Thruster is a lot faster than a single-fin and faster than a twin in all but the smallest surf. The main advantage is that you get all those bursts of speed you get with twin-fins and the speed is maintained through the turn like a single. Also the board holds in really well and it's hard to spin out . . . they're loose on the top but more positive than a twin." Kids today, he added "don't know that you can jam a turn halfway down the face or you can do a cutback under the lip." If

he'd only mentioned his trademark layback in the tube and thrown in a couple of words like "vertical" and "air," he could have been describing the pro-tour surfing of the twenty-first century. Indeed, those terms were soon in common usage among surfers, and by 1983 SURFER published photo proof of fins-out lip-pops and rail grabs— and a "Tips" article titled "Getting Air." Sure, that movement had started with the twinnies, but the Thruster accelerated the process into overdrive. There hadn't been such a burst of creative energy in the shaping room and in the waves since the shortboard revolution at the cusp of the '60s and '70s. Meanwhile, Hawaiian shaper-designer Ben Aipa (mentor to a couple of generations of Hawaii's best surfers in the '70s and '80s) correctly predicted that the era of top pros shaping their own boards was over. In the future, he said, surfers would collaborate with master shapers to further refine and advance equipment. At the time, the shapers who would be most influential—think R's Rusty Priesendorfer and Channel Island's Al Merrick— were still relatively minor figures in the industry.

For a former shaper like me, it was an incredibly exciting time to be at the helm of the magazine. I felt we really had our finger on the pulse of pro surfing and how it was impacting the advancement of surfing performance. We were calling the shots well too, correctly projecting that either Tom Carroll or Tom Curren would bring Mark Richards's four-year run of world titles to a close. It was Carroll who did so in 1983–84, during that tragic year when pro-tour politics prevented a single event from being held in Hawaii, and the world tour ended in Australia. I'd been studying the ratings-points race and realized that Carroll could earn the title by surfing (and winning) an obscure B-rated event at Deerfield Beach in Florida—one that most of the top-ranked surfers had decided not to attend since they were all Down Under. I called Carroll and found out that he planned to make a mad dash to the United States between the last two A-rated events of the season to compete, so I flew back East for the occasion. In consequence, I was the only surf mag editor and writer to witness history being made as Carroll won the contest and stole the world championship.

For the next three years, the world crown came down to a private duel between the two TCs, much like the one between Cheyne Horan and Mark Richards during the previous era. The big difference, of course, was that the Toms were both riding Thrusters. Horan stuck with his single-fins, eventually trying to elevate their performance by using a wing-keel fin he developed with America's Cup sailboat designer Ben Lexcen. But despite futuristic moves like his high-speed long-distance section floaters, his virtuoso vertical act, and his consistent contest performances (including his last major win at Sunset Beach while tripping on mushrooms in the 1989 Billabong Pro), there would be no world title for Horan, although he was runner-up four times.

In the midst of all this, SURFER's annual reader surveys showed readers were just as fascinated by surfboard design as by the surfers on the pro tour and their shapers. Design-related features consistently ranked second only to adventure travel in reader interest. As a result, in the mid-1980s, we introduced the regular monthly column "Design Forum." Surfers sent in questions that were answered by an independent expert, George Orbelian, author of *Essential Surfing*. The new department proved to be hugely popular, just as the reader surveys had suggested it would be.

That said, during SURFER's editorial meetings at that time, we were very conscious of the fact that nearly all the drama was in the realm of small-wave high-performance surfing. In Hawaii during the summer of '83, I was hanging out with staff photographer and writer Leonard Brady on the South Shore—the guy who'd introduced me to the real Hawaii, using bolt cutters to break padlocks on backcountry cane-field roads and spending happy hours hanging out in the company of exquisite, unattainable women in Hotel Street bars that had names like "Forbidden Orchid Lounge." We were talking about the way pro surfing had shifted the emphasis and focus of what it really meant to be an all-around surfer—a "waterman" in today's parlance. "Whatever happened to big-wave riding?" Leonard asked, rhetorically. "That'd be a great title for an article," I responded. "You should write it. Talk to a few of the big-wave hell-men, and let's get some balance back in the book."

That article, and a series of follow-ups—"Monster Surf" later the same year, Alec Cooke's "Kaena Point Challenge" in mid-'84, "25 Years of Big Wave Riding" in early '85, "Heli-Surfing Outside Pipeline" a few months after that, and a couple of features on some huge days at Waimea and Todos Santos—caused the pendulum to swing back strongly.

Quiksilver launched its Eddie Aikau Memorial event in 1986, providing a forum for big-wave surfing that was entirely independent of pro-tour ratings and results. As the decade drew to a close, we gave editorial space to big-wave board design, addressed the controversial issue of whether single-fins or tri-fins were best suited for big-wave guns, broke the story of Mavericks (with help from Jeff Clark, who'd surfed it as his private spot for fifteen years), and covered more early attempts at tackling the outer reefs of Oahu's North Shore. It's my belief that such coverage helped big-wave riders obtain sponsorships from companies that were otherwise focused solely on the pro tour. It also opened eyes to the fact that there were rideable 20-foot-plus waves aside from the well-known Hawaiian surf spots. It also encouraged continued R & D into gun design and led directly to tow-in surfboards and the quest to conquer waves of 40, 50, 60 feet and larger, using Jet Skis as catapults and rescue vehicles to make it possible—and survivable.

So, did SURFER set the agenda for breakthroughs in design, small-wave performance, and big-wave challenges? Or did it merely report on what was happening, perhaps even despite its coverage? The answer lies somewhere between those poles. A butterfly flaps its wings in the Amazon, causing a breeze that turns a page in an editorial office in Southern California. Oddly, that's how history was made.

opposite: TWO MAJOR TRENDS LEADING TO OPPOSITE ENDS OF THE WAVE SCALE: THE RETURN OF THE FISH, AN INDIGENOUS CALIFORNIA SPECIES OF WIDE, SPLIT-TAILED TWIN-FIN THAT MADE RIDING SMALL, LESS-POWERFUL WAVES A SNAP, AND THE INCEPTION OF TOW-IN SURFING, WHICH MADE RIDING WAVES PREVIOUSLY CONSIDERED TOO BIG TO TACKLE A REALITY. **TOM CURREN** (TOP) AND **PETE CABRINHA** (BOTTOM) DEMONSTRATE BOTH EXTREMES.

PAGE
86

BOARD COLLECTOR'S DREAM: **RENO ABELLIRA'S** STABLE OF THOROUGHBREDS, CIRCA 1975.

FUTURE SHAPES

Surfboard quivers were a relatively new concept in 1976—owning a half-dozen boards varying by mere 2-inch increments of length and infinitesimal degrees of rocker seemed beyond the realm of most mortal surfers. A major design feature in the May issue of that year reinforced this point, with the hottest young surfers on the planet posing with their excessive North Shore quivers: Shaun Tomson caressing his blue-railed Bolts and Safaris, Ian Cairns with his yellow BKs, Mark Richards with his red-and-yellow Reno wingers, Rabbit Bartholomew proudly displaying his Parrishes. These young guns brandished their big-wave battle weapons as an Indian brave might his war ponies—to this day an illuminating study on what surfers might ride on Mt. Olympus. But a glimpse at surfing's future? It wasn't the shot of Gerry Lopez and his brace of Coral Cruisers. Instead, look at the collection of Hawaii's forward-thinking Reno Abellira, shot by Jeff Divine looking straight down on it. Ignore the boards in the center, all beautiful Reno guns, but check out the two that flank his quiver. To the left, a "modern" longboard—one of the first to appear in a post-'60s magazine. And on the far right a short, winged-swallow Fish—the same twin-fin Reno rode in the 1975 Coke Contest in Australia, inspiring, with his ability to skate over flat sections in crumbly Sydney surf, an impressionable young Mark Richards. Of all the board designs depicted in this classic time capsule, only these two of Reno's are still in wide use today. ▬

ROCKET MAN

When it came to '70s surfboard design, SURFER readers tended to choose fantasy over function. What else could explain the state of West Coast surfboard design during the mid-'70s? Or more accurately, the lack of Californian surfboard designs: It seemed that everyone from Santa Cruz to San Diego was riding seven-four Island winger pintails, dreaming they'd someday experience the embarrassment of riches portrayed in all the Dick Brewer North Shore quiver shots. The thing is, what worked in 10-foot Laniakea didn't necessarily translate to 3-foot Pismo Pier. It's not like SURFER hadn't tried: A few years earlier the three-fin, venturi concave Campbell Bonzer had received major coverage, and so had the double-keeled Steve Lis Fish. But by 1977, indigenous West Coast designs were almost extinct—at least in print. Then came the Rocket Fish, a Steve Brom/Brian Gillogly/Dean Edwards–inspired design that received extravagant coverage in the July 1977 issue. At 6'4" the Rocket Fish was a full foot shorter than the average West Coast sled. But with its full template, wide point forward, split swallowtail, and twin-fins—flat foiled fins, canted, and toed in to the

nose—the Rocket Fish was so far ahead if its time that almost nobody rode it. At least not until Australian Mark Richards introduced his almost identical version of the design a year later, when just about everyone jumped on the twin. ▬

❶ CARL HAYWARD, THE BELL-BOTTOMS, BEACHCOMBER BILLS AND ROCKET FISH INDICATING IT'S 1977. ❷ HERBIE FLETCHER'S FIRST "MODERN" LONGBOARD COVER, 1976. ❸ NOAH SHIMBUKURU TAKES THE LONG WAY HOME AT PIPELINE. ❹ JEFF KRAMER, POST-MODERN LONGBOARDING, 1989.

SURFER

NOVEMBER
Vol. 17. No. 4
$1.25

Travel
Jeff Divine in Queensland:
A SURFER'S PARADISE

Action
Town and Country:
SUMMER HAWAII OVERVIEW

Evolution
New Grassroots Ideas:
DESIGN FORUM

GOING LONG

The sport was right in the middle of a major shift in surfing performance. Shaun, MR, Rabbit, PT, and Ian were doing their Free Ride thing on the North Shore, Lopez had shifted his emphasis from Pipeline to Indo but was still blowing minds in the tube, even Californians were getting rid of their beaver-tails. So during the middle of this extraordinary period of progression what was a guy on the cover of SURFER doing riding a longboard? Well first of all, it was Herbie Fletcher, figuratively one of the heaviest surfers on the planet. Second, Herbie Fletcher had already penned his epoch-bending Surfer Tip some four issues earlier: "Put a Little Lift in Your Drift," a longboarding primer that included what amounted to a declaration of independence.

"Okay now you've caught the wave early and have great position because you're on a good floater," proselytized Fletcher. *"And you're on the nose for the first time in long time 'cause it's wide, stable, and comfortable. Now, what can you do from there?"*

The surfing world would eventually answer that question by embracing, virtually en masse, what is generally termed the "modern longboard." But at the time, Herbie Fletcher's 1976 cover shot—only eight years separated SURFER longboard covers—proved that progression doesn't always mean going shorter. ▬

ALL AQUIVER

Thumb through SURFER back issues—way back—
and you'll notice that notable surfers once maintained serious relationships with their surfboards.
In the mid-'70s, for example, Kevin Naughton took
off on an around-the-world jaunt with a single Rich
Harbour pintail: orange, appearing in the pages of
SURFER being ridden in Central America as well as
North and West Africa. Those days are long gone:
Today's surf stars wheel their coffin bags around
with half a dozen or more boards stacked like Prin-
gles. We've reached the era of the disposable surfboard, at least for the pros. Requiring such finely
tuned (read "thin and extremely light") equipment,
the top talent can't afford to get seriously involved
with any one surfboard. In a recent SURFER design
feature, Hawaii's Shane Dorian explained that
during a good swell at Cloudbreak, in Fiji, a board
might last a total of three days before wearing out.
Of course very few high-level pros boards ever get
that chance: On most photo shoots in danger-
wave locations like the Mentawai Islands in Sumatra,
hard-charging surfers like Andy Irons will snap
their entire quivers. Which explains why so many
of the aforementioned SURFER shoots include the
obligatory quiver shot. It's probably the last time
we'll see any of those boards. ▬

ANDY IRONS POSES WITH HIS ULTIMATELY DOOMED
WCT QUIVER.

THE LONG AND THE SHORT OF IT

BY EVAN SLATER

EVAN SLATER

WE DIDN'T ALWAYS RIDE EVERYTHING.

Back in 1996, when I first started at SURFER, surfing was still feeling its hangover from its apartheid years. This was when—starting with the shortboard revolution and lingering well into the '90s—you were defined by your equipment: You were either a Shortboarder or a Longboarder, and never the 'twain did meet.

Still, SURFER tried to keep readers' minds open, with varying degrees of success. We told everyone "The Thrill is Back!" in 1976. We did a profile on "The Best Surfer in the World," Mike Stewart, in the early '90s. But generally, these were mere exceptions to the 6'1" squashtail thruster rule.

A couple months before I came on, we published a feature story titled "Longboarding Is Black/White/Gray." I thought the cover was atrocious—it was two shots, one of Jason Weatherly on a shortboard and one of Joel Tudor on a longboard, and they were Photoshopped together as if they were squaring off in battle. The blurb, "Can't We All Just Get Along?" also felt a bit too *National Enquirer*. But the issue sold well (shows how much I know), which meant there was still a lot of "fat, wave-hogging longboarders" and "aggro, spazzy shortboarders" looking for a resolution to the conflict. Someone had to give.

Someone *did* give that month. It was Joel Tudor, in his comments under the "Longboarding Is Gray" header. Joel was twenty at the time and generally regarded as the world's best longboarder. He was the Kelly Slater of the 9'6" plank, but there was much more to Joel than a good noseride. He emphasized that longboards weren't the answer but only part of the equation. "I'd like to see it go totally garage," he said. "Everybody has something going on. Old boards are being rediscovered and surfers are finding elements in those designs that we never should have thrown away."

And thus sprouted the Ride Everything movement. From there, films from JBrother and Thomas Campbell reminded us that longboarding was a beautiful thing, and not just for linebackers with A.P.E. gloves. From there, shortboarders expanded their templates when movies like *5'5" × 19¼"* made us realize it was okay to order shortboards that didn't look like Kelly Slater's. From there, surfboard design slowly but surely crawled out of the Dark Ages to the point where even a 12-foot battleship with a matching paddle made sense in our tool shed. As Dave Parmenter told us in his state-of-the-surfboard address at the turn of the century, "No longer is the Brewer-esque guru the controller of haute couture hemlines. The People have revolted, and, by God, if they can't find surfboards that float or paddle or glide over the flat spots, then they'll root around in the past until they cobble together a hybrid concoction that suits them."

The SURFER building itself was a microcosm of this expanding consciousness, starting with my own choice of equipment. Out in the warehouse, next to the Coke machine, Sam George's Vasa Trainer, and Jeff Divine's Trestles bike, was a board rack. And when I first started, the only type of board I placed in that rack had the following dimensions: 6'1" × 18⅛" × 2¼". I was a product of apartheid just as much as any aspiring young pro, an NSSA robot who never saw the need to go long unless it involved 20-foot Mavericks. But something profoundly changed during my time at SURFER: I discovered Doheny.

UP UNTIL THAT POINT IN MY LIFE, IT WAS THE LAST PLACE I'D HAVE CONSIDERED SURFING.

To a strict shortboarder, it's a rotten little wave. Polluted. One-quarter the size of other spots in the area. Beginners everywhere. Painfully weak. Up until that point in my life, it was the last place I'd have considered surfing. But it was the closest spot to the SURFER offices, and I had recently inherited a late '50s Dale Velzy "Easter Egg" log. I had put the board in the rack thinking it would be great for those San Onofre beach parties, but during one particularly stressful day making the Big Issue with Duke on the cover, I pulled out the Velzy at lunch and hauled it down to Doheny. There was a small south swell hitting the Boneyards section—tapered little rights running the length of the reef with all the ferocity of a petting zoo. But I paddled out anyway, fell in love with that free and easy glide, and soon made lunchtime Doheny sessions my failsafe stress-reduction therapy. The thrill, for me, had arrived.

If you flip through the publication's back issues, you'll notice that SURFER has always been at its best when it effortlessly recognizes all types of surfing. During my time at SURFER, that became much easier when I started practicing what we preached.

CHRISTIAN WACH'S ECLECTIC STABLE OF "DIFFERENT HORSES FOR DIFFERENT COURSES."

10 FEATURES THAT CHANGED THE WAY WE SURF

MEN AND THEIR MODELS. THIS 1966 "ADVERTORIAL," FEATURING DETAILS ON THE LATEST AND GREATEST SURFBOARD MODELS AT THE HEIGHT OF WHAT IS NOW KNOWN AS THE "LONGBOARD ERA," COULD BE MARGINALIZED AS NOTHING BUT A SAVVY MARKETING PLOY. CALL IT INADVERTENT, THEN, THAT IT WAS ALSO THE MOST EXTENSIVE ASSEMBLAGE OF DESIGN INFORMATION PUBLISHED AT THE TIME.

WHO WAS THIS CHILD? HE HAS NEVER EXPLAINED EXACTLY WHY HE CHOSE TO USE THAT PARTICULAR BOARD, BUT WHEN TOM CURREN PADDLED OUT ON A 5'7" TOMMY PETERSON HYDRO-HULL THRUSTER IN 15-FOOT SUMATRAN REEF SURF, IT CREATED A RIPPLE EFFECT THAT STILL RESONATES TODAY; RASTA AND ROB WOULD NEVER BE RIDING *ALAIAS* IF NOT FOR THE FREE-SPIRITED OPEN-MINDED ETHOS EXPRESSED BY THE GREAT ONE. NOT ONLY THAT, BUT THE ACCOMPANYING ARTICLE "WHO ARE THESE CHILDREN?" PENNED BY CURREN HIMSELF, IS STILL A GOOD READ.

THE BONZER. SURFBOARDS HAD BECOME ALMOST STANDARDIZED BY THE EARLY 1970s—USUALLY SOME VARIATION OF AN ISLAND-INSPIRED ROUND PIN OR DIAMOND TAIL. SO WHEN IN 1973 *SURFER* DEVOTED CONSIDERABLE EDITORIAL REAL ESTATE TO THIS WILD NEW INNOVATION—A CALIFORNIA DESIGN, AT THAT— IT TRIGGERED A NEW WAVE OF INTEREST IN SURFBOARD HYDRODYNAMICS THAT EVENTUALLY LED US TO SOME WONDERFUL PLACES.

GUNS AND HUNTERS. ONCE AGAIN *SURFER* DEMONSTRATED THE POWER OF THE PORTRAIT. ITS OCTOBER '89 ISSUE FEATURED IN-STUDIO TOM SERVAIS SHOTS OF THE BEST BIG-WAVE RIDERS IN THE WORLD POSED PROUDLY WITH THEIR HEAVY ARTILLERY. THE RESULT? A RUSH TO JOIN THE 9-FOOT-PLUS CLUB, A PUSH INTO BIG WAVES OUTSIDE OF HAWAII, EXPLORATION OF THE NORTH SHORE'S OUTER REEFS . . . TOW ROPES. AND YOU KNOW WHAT CAME AFTER THAT . . .

THE THRUSTER. THE ONLY SURFBOARD DESIGN TO EVER MAKE THE *SURFER* COVER, IN 1981, SIMON ANDERSON'S THREE-FIN THRUSTER HAD ONLY RECENTLY MADE ITS DEBUT AT THE EPIC BELLS BEACH EVENT, COVERED IN THE PREVIOUS ISSUE. ITS FEATURED PORTRAIT, HOWEVER, AND ITS HEADLINER'S ROLE IN THE MAJOR INTERIOR DESIGN FEATURE ARTICLE, DEFINITIVELY ESTABLISHED THE ULTIMATE "POWER OF THREE."

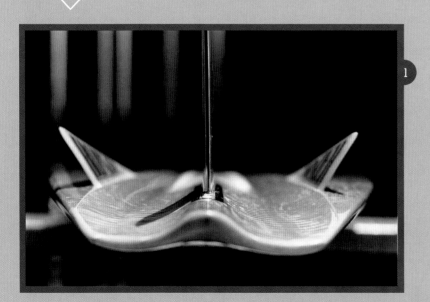

QUIVERS. WHILE NOT AN ENTIRELY NEW CONCEPT, THE IDEA OF HAVING MULTIPLE SURFBOARDS FOR DIFFERENT CONDITIONS AND MOODS WAS ILLUSTRATED IN ALL ITS GLORIOUS EXCESS WITH A PAIR OF DESIGN FEATURES IN MAY AND SEPTEMBER OF 1976. BEYOND THE EMBARRASS-MENT OF RICHES, THESE TWO ARTICLES HIGHLIGHTED A VERITABLE CORNUCOPIA OF SURFBOARD DESIGNS: STRINGERS, WINGERS, SWALLOWS, PINTAILS, FISH, MODERN LONGBOARDS . . . LITERALLY THE SHAPES OF THINGS TO COME.

JET ASSIST. LAIRD, DARRICK, AND BUZZY'S EXPLOITS WITH THE ZODIAC AND SKI ROPE HAD BEEN COVERED IN THE DECEMBER '93 ISSUE, WITH LAIRD FEATURED ON THE COVER RIDING HIS 10-FOOT BALSA. WITHIN SIX MONTHS THE STRAPPED CREW HAD CUT BOARD LENGTHS BY A THIRD, ADDED FOOT STRAPS AND LEAD WEIGHTS, AND EMBRACED THE PWC. THE *SURFER* FEATURE IN SEPTEM-BER '94 INTRODUCED THE FUTURE OF DANGER-WAVE SURFING TO A SPORT STILL DEBATING THE IMPLICATIONS OF JET-POWERED PERFORMANCE.

THE SHORTBOARD, PARTS I AND II. THE 1968 COVER STORY, FEATURING NAT YOUNG AT HONOLUA BAY, WAS AT LEAST HALF A YEAR BEHIND THE AUSSIE MAGS IN TERMS OF BREAKING THE "SHORTBOARD REVOLUTION" STORY. BUT IN TERMS OF IMPACT, THIS FEATURE, FOLLOWED BY PART TWO FOUR MONTHS LATER, PUT MORE SURFERS ON THE NEW MIND MACHINES THAN ANY OTHER.

ICONOCLAST STILL. BY THE NEW MILLENNIUM, CONTRIB-UTING WRITER DAVE PARMENTER WAS ALREADY WELL KNOWN TO *SURFER* READERS, WITH HIS WICKED COMBINATION OF EDITORIAL WIT AND VITRIOL—ONE PART OSCAR WILDE, ONE PART HOWARD BEALE FROM *NETWORK*. WHEN IT CAME TO SURFBOARD DESIGN, DAVE ALWAYS SEEMED MAD AS HELL ABOUT SOMETHING, AND IN "A REVOLUTION IS NOT A TEA PARTY" IN 2000, HE ARTICULATED A GROWING DISSATISFACTION WITH THE SURFBOARD INDUSTRY'S STATUS QUO, EFFECTIVELY SETTING THE STAGE FOR THE ERA OF "ANYTHING GOES" TO COME.

STORMY MONDAY. WHEN ON DECEMBER 5, 2005, THE VENERABLE CLARK FOAM FACTORY INEXPLICABLY SHUT ITS DOORS, THE SHOCK WAVE WAS MORE LIKE A TSUNAMI: SURFERS WHO'D NEVER EVEN CONSIDERED WHAT THEIR BOARDS WERE MADE OF WERE SUDDENLY DESPERATE FOR INFORMATION. IN 2006's "THE SHAKE-OUT," *SURFER* EDITOR CHRIS MAURO, AN ACCOMPLISHED SHAPER HIMSELF, PROVIDED A PASSIONATE PERSPECTIVE ON THE FUTURE OF OUR SACRED TOY.

① **DREW KAMPION'S** REVOLUTION BY DESIGN. ② (LEFT-RIGHT) **KEMP AABERG, MICKEY DORA** AND **JOHN PECK,** RINCON, 1966. ③ **TERRY FITZGERALD,** EARLY QUIVER PROPONENT. ④ THE REAL CORE: CLARK FOAM BEFORE THE CRASH. ⑤ THE BONZER'S VENTURI CHANNELS IN FULL RELIEF.

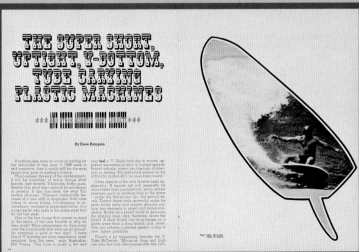
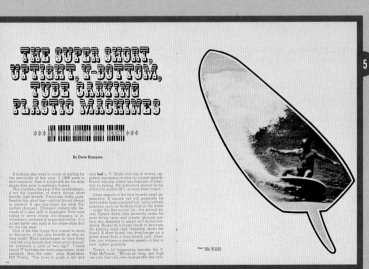

REINVENTING THE WHEEL: 5 WORST DESIGN BREAKTHROUGHS

1. **WINGED KEEL HAULED.** PADDLE OUT INTO ANY LINEUP AND YOU'RE BOUND TO FIND AT LEAST ONE LOCAL ECCENTRIC RIDING A WACKY SURFBOARD OF HIS OR HER OWN DESIGN—GENERALLY TO THE DETRIMENT OF THE SURFING EXPERIENCE. BUT NEVER HAS A TOP PROFESSIONAL SURFER SWERVED OFF THE DESIGN PATH AS SPECTACULARLY AS DID AUSTRALIA'S CHEYNE HORAN. BEGINNING IN THE MID-1980s, THE FOUR-TIME WORLD-TITLE RUNNER-UP SABOTAGED HIS OWN CAREER WITH AN INEXPLICABLE DEVOTION FIRST TO THE LAZOR ZAP, A REVERSE PUMPKIN-SEED TEMPLATE THAT TURNED NOWHERE FAST, AND EVEN MORE DISASTROUSLY TO HIS WINGED-KEEL EXPERIMENT. BOTH DESIGNS PROVED THAT WHILE HORAN WAS HOT ENOUGH TO RIP ON A BARN DOOR . . . EVEN THE DOOR WOULD'VE WORKED BETTER THAN THESE BARKERS.

2. **MIKE DOYLE'S CHEATER FIVE . . . FEET.** THERE'S ONE IN EVERY BUNCH, AND DURING THE TOM MOREY INVITATIONAL, A PROFESSIONAL NOSERIDING CONTEST HELD IN 1965, THAT ONE WAS MIKE DOYLE. THE POINT OF MOREY'S NOSERIDING EVENT WAS TWOFOLD: INTRODUCE AN OBJECTIVE TIMED JUDGING SYSTEM WHILE STIMULATING DESIGN INNOVATION. SURFERS WERE CLOCKED ON STOPWATCHES ON THE TIME SPENT ON THE FRONT THIRD OF THE BOARD. SIMPLE—UNTIL MIKE DOYLE, A TWO-TIME SURFER-POLL WINNER AND ONE OF THE SPORT'S GREAT CHAMPIONS, SHOWED UP WITH HIS HANSEN MODEL FEATURING 5 FEET OF STRINGER PROTRUDING OFF THE TAIL, EFFECTIVELY TURNING THE FRONT 4 FEET OF HIS 9'6" INTO THE NOSE. GOOD TRY, MIKE—HIS STICK WAS SUBSEQUENTLY DISQUALIFIED.

3. **A FIN BY ANY OTHER NAME.** ALMOST NO OTHER COMPONENT OF SURFBOARD DESIGN HAS BEEN MESSED WITH AS MUCH AS THE FIN. PERHAPS THAT'S BECAUSE SINCE THE ADVENT OF THE COMMERCIALLY MANUFACTURED REMOVABLE FIN BOX IN THE MID-1960s, THE FIN IS THE ONLY THING ABOUT A SURFBOARD YOU *CAN* MESS WITH. AND SO OVER THE YEARS, WE'VE SEEN THE BUTTERFLY FIN, THE TUNNEL FIN, THE FEATHERED FIN, THE KEEL FIN, THE WEIRD SWIVEL EDGE FIN . . . ONLY TO RETURN TO THE BASIC FISH DORSAL TEMPLATE THAT DESIGNERS LIKE GEORGE DOWNING AND GEORGE GREENOUGH CAME UP WITH MORE THAN FORTY YEARS AGO.

4. **TINKLERING DOWN EFFECT.** HERE'S THE THING ABOUT EFFECTIVE NEW SURFBOARD DESIGNS: SURFERS EITHER JUMP ON THEM OR THEY DON'T. RARELY HAS AN INNOVATION TAKEN YEARS TO GAIN ACCEPTANCE, AND ALMOST NEVER WITHOUT SOME SIGNIFICANT MODIFICATION. BREWER WAS MAKING TRI-FINS IN 1971, AND SO WERE THE CAMPBELL BROTHERS, BUT IT WOULD BE TEN YEARS BEFORE THE THRUSTER, IN A VERY DIFFERENT INCARNATION, STANDARDIZED THE DESIGN. THIRTY-FOUR YEARS MUST BE A RECORD, THOUGH. THAT'S HOW LONG IT'S BEEN SINCE THE TINKLER TAIL WAS INTRODUCED. BRAINCHILD OF BOB TINKLER, THE ELABORATE MECHANISM BUILT INTO THE SURFBOARD TAIL IS SUPPOSED TO PROVIDE ADJUSTABLE FLEX AT THE CLICK OF A KNOB. HOW FUNCTIONAL—AND POPULAR—IT MAY TURN OUT TO BE APPARENTLY HAS YET TO BE DETERMINED. IF ANYONE HAS EVER TRIED ONE, PLEASE LET US KNOW.

5. **KELLY SLATER'S CINDERELLA STORY.** BUT IN THIS CASE THE GLASS SLIPPER FIT ONLY THE PRINCE—HAD CINDERELLA TRIED ONE ON, SHE WOULD HAVE BEEN SITTING IN THE WATER UP TO HER CLAVICLE WITH EVERY OTHER SURFER WHO ATTEMPTED TO RIDE ONE OF THESE AL MERRICK–DESIGNED SKIMBOARDS WITH FINS. UNDER KELLY'S MAGICAL FEET, THESE EXTREMELY NARROW, LOW-VOLUME SLIVERS PROVIDED HIGH-PERFORMANCE BREAKTHROUGHS: THEY PROVED EXCEPTIONAL FOR DELIBERATELY PEARLING THE NOSE IN A TURN AND THEN RIDING BACKWARD, AND THEY ALSO FACILITATED DUCK-DIVING THROUGH CLOSEOUT SETS AT BACKDOOR PIPELINE—BOTH ATTRIBUTES COMPLETELY MEANINGLESS TO 99.999 PERCENT OF THE WORLD'S SURFERS.

following spread: **SHAUN TOMSON'S** 1975 QUIVER OF MATCHING TOM PARRISH BOLTS AND **SPIDER MURPHY** SAFARIS REPRESENTED WEALTH UNIMAGINABLE TO THE AVERAGE *SURFER* READER, FOR WHOM OWNERSHIP OF TWO SURFBOARDS WOULD HAVE BEEN CONSIDERED EXCESSIVE.

"SURFING HAS
TOO MANY
RADICAL PEOPLE."

DON HANSEN
"THE SUPER SHORT, UPTIGHT, V-BOTTOM
TUBE CARVING PLASTIC MACHINES AND
OTHER ASSORTED SHORT SUBJECTS,"
SEPTEMBER 1968

HOW WE
RIDE:

SURFER ON
PERFORMANCE

A TURN
FOR THE BETTER

IF THERE WAS A TIME WHEN SURFING PERFORMANCE DIDN'T MATTER, we've never heard of it. Ancient Hawaiian surf lore is filled with references to the expertise and flair with which eighteenth-century *he'nalu* heroes rode their *koa* and *wili-wili* boards. Once transplanted to "da Mainland," those performance parameters expanded—and don't let the sepia-tone fool you: Those early twentieth-century surfriders may have looked as though they were just standing there, but in fact they were pushing hard against performance barriers every time they paddled out. Surfboard design followed in step, not always with pure function, but with desire: to trim faster, turn quicker, ride deeper. Even a cursory look at the sport's time line will show that, whether from wood or foam, no surfer ever intentionally designed a surfboard that was wider, slower, and easier to balance. No, the goal has always been increased performance regardless of what shape that took.

By the time SURFER began publication in 1960, the sport's basic performance pattern had already been set. Those early '60s surfers, who had just

recently made the switch from balsa wood to polyurethane foam, already had the compulsories down: bottom turn, trim while moving forward on the board, backpedal to the tail, cutback into the curl . . . then repeat. While this essential choreography might seem archaic, it remains the standard today, modern weight shifts and pro-level aerials notwithstanding. But for its first few years, SURFER didn't assertively push the performance angle. The tone instead was of an editorial gathering of the tribe—as if the magazine needed a few seasons to bring everybody up to speed.

As SURFER hit its stride as a forum, its big-wave coverage was the big draw. Small wonder—it was an exciting time on Oahu's North Shore, with surfing's top fighter jocks growing bolder and bolder in the big stuff. Waimea Bay had become a spot, not merely a stunt; Sunset Beach and newly christened breaks like Laniakea were being tackled at size; the fearsome Banzai Pipeline had been board-surfed and, in Butch van Artsdalen and young John Peck's well-documented efforts, actually tuberidden. But, like the next turning point in big-wave riding some thirty years later

(when '90s hell-men first began picking up the tow rope), all this heavy water action didn't translate to the collective experience of being a surfer in, say, 1963. Waimea Bay was *Ride the Wild Surf*, when, in fact, most mortal surfers were looking for *A Cool Wave of Color*, with a focus on "real wave" performance. Phil Edwards topped the first Surfer Poll, held in 1963, his status augmented, no doubt, by the strength of his performances in the period's surf films. Bruce Brown's *Surfing Hollow Days*, especially, depicted the lanky, laconic regularfoot from Oceanside as the total package: Edwards is shown ripping all sorts of average surf, cranking cutbacks, stalling in the curl, and riding the nose. And he *was* the first guy to paddle out and surf Pipeline: A sequence of his epic second ride ran in the April '63 issue.

Strange, then, that what characterized the mid-'60s performance paradigm was the noseride. In defense of a good noseride, it was functional (in the case of the tricky Strauch Stretch, erroneously dubbed the "cheater five," extremely so), in almost all scenarios difficult as well as stylish, favoring a dancer's approach,

ROOKIE *SURFER* PHOTO EDITOR JASON MURRAY SHOT THIS **BRUCE IRONS** AERIAL DURING THE 2000 OP PRO BOAT TRIP CHALLENGE IN INDONESIA. UNFORTUNATELY MURRAY WAS STANDING IN A BOAT NEXT TO VETERAN PHOTOG TOM SERVAIS, WHOSE ALMOST-IDENTICAL VERSION (IT WAS A TAD TIGHTER) ULTIMATELY MADE THE COVER.

preceding spread: **CLAY MARZO**, FINS—AND MIND—TOTALLY FREE.

as opposed to a fighter's. Noseriding facilitated major design progression—the concave "noserider" representing the sport's first truly specialized surfboard innovation since the Hot Curl proto-gun. And the noseride made good copy—it was the Stale Fish aerial of its time, and just like today's aerial was tailor-made for still photography. Which is why photos of David Nuuhiwa, like the one on the July '66 cover, epitomized performance as definitively as did Jordy Smith's frontside rail grab 360-degree cover shot in February '09. Jordy Smith is a fantastic all-around surfer—so was David Nuuhiwa—but since noseriding's mid-'60s heyday it's been the magazine's peak action shot. So trim was out, turn was in, and it was for that maneuver in all its variations that in the late 1960s surfers adopted a term that has now become cliché: radical. Top turn, cutback, roller-coaster, off-the-lip, roundhouse, snapback, gouge, frontside air, backside air, tailslide, reverse. With a big enough thumb you could use bound back-issues

of SURFER as a flip book, flickering through the decades to see the history of surfing appear in sequence.

And what a highlight reel it would be: Nat at Ocean Beach, then Haleiwa; Jock at Pipe; Gerry at Ala Moana, then Pipe; Sammy and Owl on Huge Monday; Terry Fitz at Narrabeen; John Van Ornum at Newport Point; Larry Bertlemann at Kaisers; Reno at Sunset; Fitzy at J-Bay; Shaun, Rabbit, and the Free Ride crew at Pipe and Off-the-Wall; Herbie on the nose; Russ Short at Pelican Point; PT soul arching; Ian snapping back; Buttons at V-Land; Dane powering; MR twinning; Cheyne on his McCoys; Kwock at Echo Beach; Simon at Big Bells; Tom Carroll everywhere; Tom Curren ripping Rincon; Martin Potter at the Bay of Plenty; Occy on fire; Kong at the West Peak; Freida on tour; Parsons at Todos; Occy versus Curren; Christian boosting at Lowers; Curren's comeback; Lisa's top turns; Kelly at the Cabo Classic; Kelly at Lowers; Kelly

at Pipeline and Backdoor; Kelly at Lances; Curren at J-Bay; Benji's Backyard; Mel at Mavs; the Strapped Crew at Peahi; Occy's comeback; Tudor's throwback; the Andy and Bruce Show; Laird at Teahupoo; Dorian at Teahupoo; Kelly switching feet at Padang-Padang; Kelly taking Trestles; Kelly paipo boarding Backdoor; Jordy, Dane, Clay, Dusty, Carissa, Stephanie, John John, Brother, Ford, and all the other young guns who will provide SURFER with peak moments of performance well into the next century.
—SG

❶ JOHN SEVERSON''S SEQUENCE OF **JOHN PECK'S** SEMINAL GRUB-RAIL TUBE HINTED AT PIPELINE PERFORMANCE TO COME. ❷ *SURFER* PHOTOGRAPHER SCOTT AICHNER'S ANNUAL TRIP TO NORTH CAROLINA'S OUTER BANKS IS AT LEAST PARTIALLY RESPONSIBLE FOR A MAJOR EASTERN PERFORMANCE JUMP—ESPECIALLY IN THE TUBE. **JESSE HINES.** ❸ **RABBIT BARTHOLOMEW,** MOMENTS AFTER A BROKEN LEASH COST HIM WORLD TITLE NUMBER TWO IN 1979. ❹ **JOEL TUDOR** CHAMPIONED THE RETRO MOVEMENT WITH PURE STYLE. ❺ **LAYNE BEACHLEY,** SEVEN-TIME WORLD CHAMPION AND THE MOST POWERFUL ALL-AROUND PERFORMER IN WOMEN'S SURFING. ❻ **JOEL PARKINSON,** WINNING IN FRONT OF HOMETOWN GOLD COAST FANS. 2006.

❶ SHANE DORIAN IS STRAIGHT UP THE SPORT'S TOP PERFORMER IN EVERYTHING FROM 6 FOOT TO 60. ❷ THE SOUL ARCH (PERFORMED BY ALEX KOPPS) STILL FEELS SO RIGHT, ❸ EVEN IN THE AGE OF AERIAL (AS PERFORMED BY JAMIE O'BRIEN). ❹ THE FEBRUARY 1972 ISSUE OF *SURFER* FEATURED A GLEN CHASE ILLUSTRATION OF A SURFER DOING A CARVING BACKSIDE 360 ALMOST IDENTICAL TO THIS ONE BY BOBBY MARTINEZ, THIRTY-SIX YEARS LATER. ❺ DAVID NUUHIWA, DEFINING TOP—AND TIP— FORM IN 1965.

"THERE ARE SO MANY GOOD SURFERS TODAY THAT ALMOST ANY DAY AT ALMOST ANY BEACH CAN BLOW YOUR MIND. THERE ARE GUYS OUT THERE ON THE FRINGES OF MAGAZINELAND WHO HAVE CONTRIBUTED EVERY BIT AS MUCH TO THE ARTISTIC WEALTH OF THE UNIVERSE AS VAN GOGH, HERMANN HESSE, OR INGMAR BERGMAN. SOME ARE EVEN CLOSING IN ON THE DYLAN."

DREW KAMPION
"STYLE: A COMMON MAN'S LOOK AT ARTISTIC WHOLES," DECEMBER 1971

opposite: CONTEMPORARY PERFORMERS LIKE **JOEL PARKINSON** TOOK SURFING INTO THE CLOUDS, AND *SURFER* PRESENTED THE RESULTS WITH DEFINITIVE PHOTO SEQUENCES LIKE THIS.

FASHIONABLY LATE BLOOMER

BY CHRIS MAURO

I OBSERVED KELLY'S PENDING DEPARTURE FROM THE ASP TOUR AS AN OPPORTUNITY TO END THE PERFORMANCE CRISIS.

Let me begin with a sobering admission: I didn't care much for Kelly Slater's brand of surfing throughout most of the '90s. How my sacrilege didn't prevent me from landing a stint at SURFER in the summer of 1998 still puzzles me. Kelly, after all, was just getting ready to claim his sixth world title—his fifth straight—topping Mark Richards's record that was once thought invincible. The generational jihad waged by Slater's New School followers had decimated the ranks of the older Curren Era crowd, sending a number of former greats into personal tailspins. But after capturing the sport's most esteemed record, Slater vowed that he'd hang up his jersey. Fans of progressive surfing reeled: Slater was so far ahead of his contemporaries that any future without him seemed pale, gray, and devoid of meaning. The sport was poised to drift aimlessly, with design and performance drifting along as a result.

Though I'd miss his presence too, as a surfboard shaper, I felt that Kelly's "retirement" might not be such a bad thing, opening the design doorway a crack to let in some logic, which seemed to have vanished during the course of the decade. As ridden by the phenomenal Slater, the super-narrow, hyper-rockered, anorexic Al Merrick chips of choice were the culmination of twenty-five years of shortboard refinement: the new gold standard. Yet the valuation was based on pure illusion. Tom Curren summed it up best when he said Kelly's boards were like Cinderella's glass slippers, "And Kelly is the only one who can make them work."

Curren's remark hadn't slowed the masses from following Kelly's lead. After all, Curren defined old-school values at a time when Kelly's new-school dogma was the orthodoxy du jour. Soon Slater-inspired chips could be found in every surf shop board rack like toothpicks in a box. His fellow pros followed blindly down the same path, desperately giving chase, while "cutting edge" performance devolved into hydrodynamic failure and recovery. Yet everyone in the surf industry, including shapers who knew better, seemed happy to partake in the performance Ponzi scheme. The period's surf video editors didn't help, with their repetitive blend of punk music and trick inventories, desktop trash bins filled with the other ninety-nine failed attempts. Don't get me wrong, the new-school generation was certainly breaking new ground, laying a solid foundation for much of today's remarkable above-the-lip acrobatics, but speed and power surfing had taken a huge step backward in the process. Those who actually preferred surfing on the wave's face, a.k.a. the vast majority, were left struggling on toothpicks.

By the mid-'90s, most of the surfing population was holding one of these toxic assets under their arm. Not since the early '70s, when bad acid tabs were fueling the fledgling shortboard revolution, had the bulk of the surfing population been so underserved by their equipment. Simply pumping down the line required hard labor. If the reflexes weren't razor sharp, if the feet weren't in the perfect sweet spot, if you breached even the slightest flat spot along the way, it was welcome to Bogtown. The gap between the average surfer's wants and true needs was never bigger—we'd become a global tribe of surfboard fashion victims.

So although it ran in direct opposition to a sport held in Slater's thrall, I observed Kelly's pending departure as an opportunity to end the performance crisis. To that end, I felt it was a great time to join the crew at the magazine—I was going to help lead the sport in a new direction.

A year into my new gig, I got my chance, when I convinced Kelly to make a trip to the Mentawais for what was envisioned as an all-star session. Kelly, who'd actually followed through with his early retirement plan, found himself working harder than ever doing promos and was in desperate need of a real vacation. As predicted, none of Kelly's running mates had been able to fill his shoes—that was left to the previous generation. Out on tour, the Old School was

making a comeback: Mark Occhilupo's remarkable return from the fat farm was the story of the year. Close second was Tom Curren, who was busy playing the Chuck Yeager test-pilot role and experimenting with new equipment. His tiny "Fireball Fish" experiment in serious Sumatran surf was a shocking glimpse into the future, though it would take several years to fully penetrate conventional wisdom.

My idea for the Mentawais trip, which took months of haggling with agents and managers to pull off, was to mix generations and equipment together in the remote idyllic Indonesian surf and then compare notes. Occy, Curren, Brad Gerlach, and Luke Egan were to be contrasted with Slater, Rob Machado, Shane Dorian, and Ross Williams. All these guys were at—or at least nearing— the top of their game, and documenting this moment in time would be a very fleeting opportunity. Unfortunately, on the day of departure, Curren and Occy both pulled out—the crisis in East Timor was heating up, and I guess traveling to a war zone seemed a little dicey to these two married men. I was devastated. With two of my three central characters missing, I had to change the angle of my story. Heeding editor Steve Hawk's suggestion, I called it "Tomorrowland" and focused on where these guys were headed.

Of course the big question at the time was whether Kelly would return to competition. When I finally got around to asking him for the record, it was late at night, and we were conducting an interview on the floor of our cramped, dimly lit sleeping quarters aboard *Neptune 1*. When he paused, sighed, and gazed at the toes stretched out in front of him before replying, I already had my answer. As I saw it, until somebody came along who could truly threaten to put Slater in the rear view mirror, he'd get more out of challenging himself . . . on a golf course.

Kelly's surfing on the Tomorrowland trip was superb, the photos and film depicting a surfer so confident in his abilities that he made the other fantastic performers look, if not exactly second rate, at least part of the pack. Still, watching him, you got the feeling Slater was gathering himself for something, waiting for some new challenge to arise.

As it turned out, Andy Irons was just what Kelly was waiting for. Irons's first world title, which came three years into Slater's hiatus, was widely billed as the passing of the torch. Andy, along with peers like Mick Fanning, Joel Parkinson, and Andy's brother Bruce, were fusing the best of old- and new-school doctrines. What's more, Andy was the anti-Slater. He partied. He got pissed. And he wasn't the least bit media savvy or, for that matter, intimidated by Slater. Their rivalry was very real. Kelly's return, as expected, caused mass hysteria, something Irons didn't care for. They had run-ins both in and out of the water, privately and publicly, fueling the intensity of their heated title showdown of 2003. Never before had two surfers been so evenly matched. By taking the title in the last event of the year, at Pipeline no less, Andy spearheaded what was now perceived as a "Post-Slater Era." His back-to-back titles coincided with repeat Surfer Poll victories—which had been Slater's private domain for the previous decade—meaning he'd also successfully captured the hearts and minds of the general public. When Andy ran away easily with his third straight title, Kelly was seething.

One of Andy's premier shapers, Eric Arakawa, was at the forefront of shaping technology during Andy's climb up the ranks. An open-minded innovator, Eric made HIC the first major board label to utilize shaping software via the Surf CAD (Computer Aided Design). While I was researching the concept for a "Design

CHRIS MAURO (RIGHT) WITH CURRENT *SURFER* EDITOR IN CHIEF JOEL PATTERSON.

Forum" article in 1999, Eric let me shape a board on his computer in his home office. "Design Forum" was my favorite column to work on, mostly because I'd shaped just over a thousand boards before joining the magazine. I considered Eric and his ilk the sages of our tribe, and I felt extremely fortunate that their doors were open to me. I was privy to a lot of pet projects. That day was a prime example. And the magnitude of the breakthrough was obvious: This was the future. Everything about the board could be measured, altered, and viewed from various angles on screen. The tools allowed the user to remove bumps, fix curves, and change dimensions midstream. There was no more shooting in the dark or scanning and copying required.

CAD technology would play a huge role in the fledgling surfboard renaissance. Because it came with a new machine that cut boards to order, labels were liberated from ordering identical models in bulk. Before CADs, these same labels rarely strayed from their most popular designs. Each had a small set of plugs, or pre-shapes, that came off a machine in a separate factory before being shipped to their headquarters where they would be finished by a ghost shaper. Though minor tweaks could be made to these plugs, the surf-shop racks were as homogenized as they had been during the popout craze of the mid-'60s.

During Slater's hiatus, the masses slowly started drifting toward more pragmatic equipment. Occy and Irons were both riding meatier boards, which helped reverse the trend of the incredible shrinking surfboard. A grassroots hybrid revolt was well under way in various pockets, with guys like Curren, Cory Lopez, and Chris Ward opening eyes. As more and more designers yanked forgotten templates out of their attics and began applying modern foils, all things old were suddenly new again. By the time Slater returned to the fray and recaptured the world title in 2005, a full-blown retro revival was under way, beavertails and all. While some of it was absurd, the public had nonetheless wised up and had no intention of rejoining Slater on his toothpicks. Besides, the closure of Clark Foam dwarfed Slater's return to the top as a news and design story at the end of 2005. While the immediate fallout of the closure was decidedly negative, it forced designers to dig deep, open their minds, and experiment in order to survive.

When Slater begrudgingly handed the crown to Fanning in 2007, the assumption was he'd ride off into the sunset again—only something happened on the way to the horizon. Spending his off season in Santa Barbara, he finally relented and began participating in the surfboard renaissance in California's lineups. By pushing himself out of his comfort zone, Slater discovered what everyone else already knew: that experimentation eventually led to new levels of performance—and fun.

Riding quad-fins, round-nose pods, and a variety of fish-inspired derivatives, Slater unleashed hidden secrets of drive, power, maneuverability, and flow. By the time he arrived in Australia in the spring of 2008 for his obligatory cameo at the Quiksilver Pro, he had transformed his competition boards for the first time in more than a decade. From his first heat, it was obvious Slater's new board was setting him apart from the herd. Where others were laboring, he was flowing on his shorter, stubbier board. Some eighteen years after his first world-title quest began, at age thirty-six he went on to smash the competition and repeated the process five more times on the way to his tenth world title, bookending my ten years at SURFER. My opinion of Slater had come full circle.

The reason I hadn't been able to wait for him to disappear the first time around was because I'd spent the better part of five years in surf shops and shaping rooms on the central coast of California, a place where the renaissance had been percolating early (a whole other story). And frankly, while consoling customers in need of equipment intervention and recovery programs was a very profitable and rewarding business, the suffering had to stop. Slater fashion had been killing careers.

So on the matter of surfboards, I'll admit, I came to SURFER with an agenda, which was to convince the surfing world that when it came to our equipment, we were sinking, and quite literally. I feel like a worn-out record now, having cranked the same tune for more than a decade. But I'll be damned if Kelly didn't provide the best going-away gift ever by finally heeding the call. So what if he was fashionably late to this party. The guy still lit up the room, validating the entire movement in one beautiful record-setting swoop.

A few days after Kelly clinched his title, I was on the phone with Australia's Mark Richards talking—surprise—about design. He was raving about how Kelly's surfing reached an entirely new pinnacle on equipment that finally matched his abilities. Apparently, he'd been waiting just as long to see that day. We're both pretty sure Kelly will have to retire eventually, but now, all of a sudden, a future without him really does look pale, gray, and devoid of meaning.

KELLY SLATER, WITH A LITTLE MORE FIN AND A LOT LESS HAIR THAN WHEN HE WON HIS
FIRST WORLD TITLE IN 1992, IS STILL THE BEST SURFER IN ANY OCEAN.

Like time lapse photography, SURFER covers provide a fascinating portrait of the sport's ever-changing performance standards, from the very first turn to the very latest aerial maneuver. And while the era-defining cover shots haven't always been action oriented—the occasional empty wave, artsy collage, and significant portrait making periodic appearances—the hallowed space at the front of the book has traditionally been reserved for the state-of-the-art turn, cutback, tube, and big wave drop. The fifty-year evolution of each category mapped out, so to speak, on first a bimonthy then a monthly basis; when it comes to surfing performance, SURFER literally has it covered. ▬

TURN

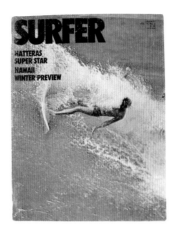
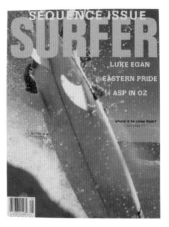
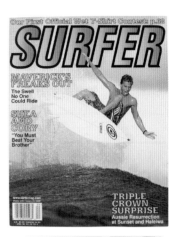

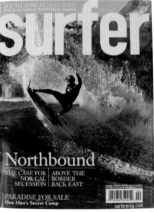

TUBE RIDE

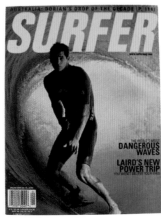

CUTBACK

  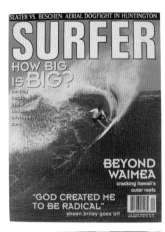 

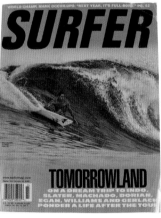   

BIG WAVE

 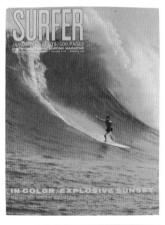  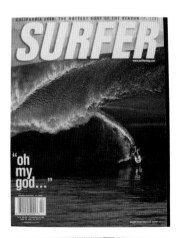

   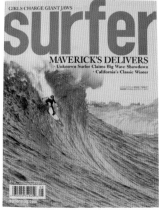

TURN FOR THE BETTER

Believe it or not, the first surfing maneuver didn't appear on the cover of SURFER until 1964—four years into the magazine's publishing run. And the Phil Edwards cutback featured on the July issue that year was indeed the prototypical turn: More cutbacks have made the cover of SURFER than any other maneuver. However, comprising only 6.43 percent of SURFER covers, the cutback, along with periodically updated versions of the roller coaster (first seen in March '68), has still taken a backseat to the tuberide— by an overwhelming percentage the most popular cover image. We can trust the tuberide, it seems—we ride along in our imaginations. But for the maneuver we require proof. Consider the period that separated the very first cover featuring an aerial—Larry Bertlemann in March '84—from the second—Christian Fletcher in December '88—a full four years. SURFER's readers obviously didn't trust the single aerial image until they had seen sequences of surfers actually pulling off the high-flying feat. And nobody did that more consistently—and with more aplomb—than San Clemente's Christian Fletcher.

OH MY GOD

It was like nothing we'd ever seen before. When in June of 2002 Laird Hamilton, the Maui Surf Muscle, told SURFER editors he planned to chase a big south swell to Tahiti with the express purpose of towing into the fearsome left tube at Teahupoo, a few eyebrows were raised. After all, the relatively new discipline of jet-assisted tow-in surfing had previously been applied mostly to five-story, offshore reef breaks—not dredging, bottomless, backless barrels. But Hamilton clearly declared his major. "I think you can take off a lot deeper at Teahupoo," he claimed, "and come into the tube from behind the peak." Sure, Laird. Some weeks later, rumors began circulating that Laird had, in fact, connected with a major Tahitian swell event—and with tow-rope in hand. The SURFER staff awaited photographic results with, if not exactly skepticism, a measure of good-natured anticipation. Then the first image of "The Ride" appeared. "Oh my god!" This first from photo department, then the editorial department, then the art department . . . the receptionist, warehouse manager, and virtually everyone else who beheld it. Always the same response, delivered wide-eyed and slack-jawed while gaping at the single most incredible image ever submitted to SURFER magazine: Laird Hamilton at Teahupoo, absolutely redefining "rideable," transforming what for the previous fifty years had been a rather timid approach to dangerous waves into the modern realm of stunt surfing. Welcome to Planet Slab.

❶ HIGH-FLYING CHRISTIAN FLETCHER, 1987. ❷ LAIRD HAMILTON'S EPOCH-BENDING TEAHUPOO TUBE. ❸ PREVIOUSLY UNRIDDEN AUSTRALIAN "SLABS" ARE POPPING UP IN EVERY ISSUE THESE DAYS.

POWER SURFING

There was precedent. *Ka'a wele:* the ancient Hawaiian art of "canoe leaping," in which privileged (and undoubtedly sponsored) *alii* would be paddled into blue-water breaks like Waikiki's Kalehuawehe by a six-man outrigger canoe and step off onto their *olos* with speed enough to beat the fastest breaker. Funny how this innovation was overlooked for a century or two; even more curious how slowly big-wave surfing actually progressed in the second half of the twentieth century. In the 1963 film *Ride the Wild Surf*, main character Jody Wallis (played by Fabian, with stunt work by Mickey Dora) won the contest at Waimea Bay by paddling into the biggest set wave, making it to the bottom, and edging out onto the shoulder. In 1990, Hawaiian waterman Keone Downing won the "Eddie" at Waimea doing pretty much the same thing. So when during the 1992 "Eddie" big-wave riders Laird Hamilton, Buzzy Kerbox, and Darrick Doerner eschewed the scrum at the Bay to whip themselves into clean 18-footers at Backyard Sunset from behind Kerbox's Zodiac, SURFER got towed right along with them. A helicopter image of the Jet Age's seminal session (shot by Sylvain Casenave) was immediately featured on the cover. While the rest of the surfing world debated the ethics of grabbing the throttle, SURFER continued to feature—and in many cases champion—the sport's first actual quantum leap in surfing technique since the days of *ka'a wele*. ▬

GREAT GROMS

In January of 1969, Wayne Lynch, the sixteen-year-old wunderkind of Australian surfing had his U.S. coming-out with a splashy SURFER profile written by Aussie journalist John Witzig. Lynch was called an "International Man," his radical, multidirectional performances on the newly dubbed "shortboard" upstaging even the great Nat Young. He appeared almost super-natural to the American readers who had only recently wired the noseride. Yet only nine years later, another Wayne Lynch profile by Witzig appeared, titled "Wayne Lynch at 25," marveling at how hardcore the "Lorne Fish" still was at that advanced age. This was, of course, long before the era of thirty-seven-year-old world champions. But SURFER has always been keen to introduce the next generation of surf stars, This is evidenced by the continuing popularity of "Surfer's Hot 100," a special feature profiling the sport's hottest young talent that debuted in October of 1982—and remains the sport's main scouting report for aspiring pros. Because while SURFER might not these days relegate a twenty-year-old ripper to "lion in winter" status, it still enjoys watching tomorrow's surfing today. ▬

opposite: DARRICK DOERNER, PEAHI PARADIGM SHIFTER.
above: WAYNE LYNCH, BENDING VECTORS, CIRCA 1968.

TOP 10 SURFERS OF ALL TIME

1. **KELLY SLATER.** THE GREATEST? DEBATABLE. THE BEST? NO QUESTION. WHEN IT COMES TO SHEER PERFORMANCE—IN EVERYTHING FROM 2-FOOT COCOA BEACH TO WAIMEA BAY—NO OTHER SURFER HAS EVEN COME CLOSE. WITH ALMOST AS MANY WORLD TITLES AS HE HAS FINGERS, YOU COULD EXCUSE SLATER IF HE RESTED ON A FEW LAURELS. BUT THE FACT THAT HE IS STILL SETTING PERFORMANCE STANDARDS, STILL HUGELY INFLUENTIAL IN CONTEMPORARY SURFBOARD DESIGN, AND STILL LEADING THE WAY WHILE INTO HIS THIRD DECADE OF SURF STARDOM CLINCHES HIS SPOT ATOP THIS ROSTER.

2. **LAIRD HAMILTON.** TOW-IN SURFING, MEGA-SLAB RIDING, STAND-UP PADDLE, THE FOIL BOARD: NO SURFER IN MODERN HISTORY HAS INTRODUCED AS MANY NEW WAYS TO RIDE WAVES—AND ACHIEVED TOTAL MASTERY IN EACH DISCIPLINE—AS HIS LAIRDNESS. SIMPLY THE GREATEST.

3. **GERRY LOPEZ.** OKAY, SO HE WAS NO GREAT CONTEST-SURFER, AND HIS BACKSIDE WAS SOFT. BUT PUT HIM IN HOLLOW, GNARLY LEFTS—MOST NOTABLY THE BANZAI PIPELINE—AND LOPEZ'S PRETERNATURAL COOL ELEVATED OUR OFTEN VIOLENT ACT INTO ART.

4. **NAT YOUNG.** THERE WERE MANY GREAT CHAMPIONS DURING THE "LONGBOARD ERA" BUT NONE LIKE "THE ANIMAL" WHO, WHEN IT CAME TO RIDING BOARDS IN THE 9-FOOT RANGE, DID EVERYTHING BETTER THAN ANYONE ELSE. OH, AND THEN THERE WAS THAT WHOLE "SHORT-BOARD" THING . . .

5. **LAYNE BEACHLEY.** WHY NOT LISA ANDERSEN? OR MARGO GODFREY OBERG OR FREIDA ZAMBA, FOR THAT MATTER? BECAUSE NO OTHER FEMALE SURFER HAS PROVEN HERSELF SO VERSATILE, SO DETERMINED, SO SUCCESSFUL, AND YET SO RELENTLESSLY "HER OWN MAN" AS HAS MS. BEACHLEY.

6. **TOM CURREN.** HIS RAPPORT WITH THE WAVES BORDERED ON THE MIRACULOUS, BUT THEN WHAT WOULD YOU EXPECT FROM A CARPENTER'S SON? STYLE, COMMITMENT, COURAGE, AND A TOUCH OF MYSTERY—CURREN PERSONIFIED THE GLOBALLY ACCEPTED PERFORMANCE PARAMETERS.

7. **SHAUN TOMSON.** THE 1977 WORLD CHAMP OFTEN GETS LUMPED IN WITH THE REST OF HIS "FREE RIDE" COHORTS. BUT THE TRUTH IS THAT FOR THOSE FEW TORRID SEASONS ON THE NORTH SHORE, WHEN IT CAME TO REDEFINING THE TUBERIDE, TOMSON WAS MILES AHEAD OF HIS STELLAR CONTEMPORARIES. PROBABLY STILL IS.

8. **MARK RICHARDS.** IF THE WOUNDED GULL HAD BEEN ANY GOOD AT BACKSIDE TUBERIDING AT PIPELINE, HE'D PROBABLY BE NUMBER SEVEN. AS IT IS, THIS FOUR-TIME WORLD CHAMPION AND TWIN-FIN INNOVATOR WILL JUST HAVE TO BE REMEMBERED AS ONE OF THE MOST DOMINANT, VERSATILE COMPETITORS EVER TO SLIP ON A COLORED JERSEY.

9. **TOM CARROLL.** AS AN EIGHTEEN-YEAR-OLD ROOKIE, HE MADE THE FINALS OF THE 1979 PIPELINE MASTERS, AND TODAY, TWO WORLD TITLES, TWENTY-SIX CAREER WINS, THREE PIPE MASTERS VICTORIES, AND THREE DECADES LATER, HE'S TOWING INTO HORRENDOUS OUTER REEF SLABS SOMEWHERE IN THE SOUTHERN OCEAN. NEED WE SAY ANYTHING MORE?

10. **ANDY IRONS.** THE PAST TWO DECADES HAVE PRODUCED ONLY THREE TRULY GREAT SURFERS. ANDY IS ONE OF THEM. SUPREMELY POISED IN DANGER-WAVES, ELECTRIFYING IN THE SMALL STUFF, DISCIPLINED ENOUGH TO HAVE A COUPLE OF WORLD TITLES ATTACHED TO HIS NAME, BUT STILL WILD ENOUGH TO MAKE PEOPLE WANT TO DRESS LIKE HIM—SURF STARDOM PERSONIFIED.

BREAKING
MAVERICKS

BY BEN MARCUS

BEN MARCUS, SANTA CRUZ, 1980.

WE CAN OPEN PANDORA'S BOX OR KEEP IT SHUT.

Half Moon Bay was the surfing-world joke of the North Coast during the 1970s, a place of pumpkins and bumpkins, even worse than Pacifica—a town farther north whose surf scene usually consisted of two guys in cutoff Levi's strapping their boards the wrong way to the roof of a Camaro to hightail it back to Fremont. Half Moon Bay wasn't a happening place in the '70s, which is probably why I stayed with my mom in Santa Cruz when my parents got divorced. Santa Cruz had Pleasure Point, the Rivermouth, the Harbor, and everything else. Half Moon Bay had Princeton Jetty—usually lackluster and occasionally great—and the beachbreaks running down from it, and that was it—or so the world thought.

During the '70s, my mom would drive from Santa Cruz up to the restaurant/gas station at Gazos Creek—known as Pinkie's at the time—and hand me off to Pops, who lived in Moss Beach,

right there on the corner of Airport Road and Los Banos. This was a dangerous place to live sometimes, because Airport Road was at the time a gravel straightaway that paralleled the landing strip at Half Moon Bay Airport. Local yahoos would get tanked up on Boone's Farm Strawberry Hill or Ripple or whatever and use Airport Road as a drag strip. More than a few times, those Don "The Snake" Prudhomme wannabes in their Z28s and GTOs would blow the transition from gravel to pavement, lift off, get serious air, and land in my dad's front yard.

From my dad's house, my younger brother and I could ride motorcycles illegally up Los Banos, past the Moss Beach Distillery, and along the cliffs overlooking the Fitzgerald Marine Reserve to an empty area my big brother called Bullet Shell Ridge. There were big divots out there that looked like bomb craters, and they were fun to ride in and around and come flying out of—even on a step-through Honda 50. From the cliffs, the view of the deep, dark blue ocean and empty beaches all the way to Ross' Cove and the tip of Pillar Point was spectacular.

Riding around on Bullet Shell Ridge during the winter, it was impossible to miss a beastly lump of a wave, breaking well up past Ross' Cove, a left that wrapped around the north side of Pillar Point. Ross' Cove was doable in the '70s, but this other wave was out of the question at the time. As seen from the north side, it was a giant, gaping left that threw out hollow and then slammed shut—a monstrosity. I rode around Bullet Shell Ridge often but never saw anyone out there. The wave was unnerving to look at, like watching dinosaurs clashing far off in the distance from the top of a cliff.

I still have an undeveloped roll of Super 8 film in my garage marked "Ross' Cove," shot with my trusty Canon Super 8 with the big lens (I could never afford a Beaulieu—the Cadillac of Super 8s). Although I wrote "Ross' Cove" on the side of the cartridge, the truth is, I was shooting that big nasty clamshell barrel breaking in the no-man's-land, halfway out to the buoy. The place didn't even have a name. Or so I thought.

Toward the end of the '70s I bought a hot dog wagon on the beach in Santa Cruz called Surfer Dog. I had a concession with the State Parks Department to sell hot dogs and cold drinks on a beach that was called Twin Lakes Beach, Seabright Beach, or Castle Beach, depending on who you talked to. Surfer Dog was a good business. At the time, it was legal to bring alcohol onto the beach, and it was superpopular with people from the valley who would flock over to Santa Cruz on summer weekends, or any day that the valley was too hot and smoggy to be tolerated. Whenever I hear Van Halen's "Jamie's Crying," I can smell the mustard and the Coppertone.

Surfer Dog sponsored a baseball team that was manned by the state park rangers and lifeguards: Bob Dunker, Roger Rodd, Lynn Swank, Rod Ortiz, Alex Peabody, and two guys named Joe Clark. One of the Joe Clarks had an absolute rocket for an arm, but he was a little wild. When one of his throws broke the nose of a guy standing in the other dugout, the City of Santa Cruz put up a high fence that is still there at DeLaveaga.

Another player on the Surfer Dog team was surfer Tom Powers, a state parks lifeguard at the time and very connected with the Santa Cruz hardcore. He was a made man with the West Siders, and I was a guy only recently moved over from the valley—a Seabright midtown guy who mostly surfed Pleasure Point. But I sponsored the baseball team and flowed a lot of orange juices and sodas, and so the nicer West Side guys like Powers would talk to me, sort of.

In the '70s and '80s, surf stars were mostly Hawaiians, South Africans, and Australians. California didn't produce international surf stars back then. But growing up, I had seen many good surfers around Santa Cruz—Gene Page, Richard Schmidt, Harbor Bill, Vince Collier, and especially Kevin Reed. These guys got a little bit of attention from the likes of Kookson, Bob Barbour, and Dan Devine, but never enough, in my opinion.

My own road took a dramatic turn in 1989 when I wrote a surf-travel story about Mundaka and The Bootmaker's Daughter called "You Wouldn't Read About It" and sent it to SURFER magazine. I wrote the story from Austin, Texas, where I was trying to write a movie about an Australian kid who plays high school football. This was the first story I had submitted to a magazine, but they ran it and paid me $450, which was doubly great.

Based on that story, I was hired at SURFER and moved down to San Clemente. At the time, there were still only two major surf magazines in North America—SURFER and *Surfing*. No *Transworld, Surfer's Journal, Surfline*, or Internet at all. Getting an editorial job at a surf magazine was a big deal, like getting a seat on the New York

Stock Exchange. You didn't apply—someone had to die or get arrested. I don't remember whose seat I filled at SURFER, but I do remember what a big adventure it was to move all the way down to Orange County from Santa Cruz. I went there pretty jazzed to have a paying job writing about surfing. But I was also on a mission: to put Santa Cruz and Northern California on the map and do justice to all those people I had grown up with—even if a lot of them were obnoxious dickheads who never offered to pay for Cokes.

It was a heady honor and a big deal to be working at SURFER with guys like Jeff Divine, Steve Pezman, Paul Holmes, and Matt Warshaw. To me it was as good as getting hired at the *New Yorker*. I did my best to direct attention toward the areas I knew best, from our beloved Shark's Cove on the east side to those frightening waves I saw breaking out in front of Playland at Ocean Beach in San Francisco as a kid.

This was the mood I brought to the Action Sports Retailer trade show in San Diego in 1991. There I ran into Tom Powers, and it was nice to see someone from the Old Country in the midst of a convention center filled with everything "Down South." Powers had a strange look on his face, like he was concealing a great secret, and, in fact, right after he said hello, he held his coat open covertly, like a flasher, and revealed a VHS

above: THANKS TO COMPREHENSIVE COVERAGE OF EVERY SINGLE MAVERICKS SWELL, THE ANONYMITY ONCE EXPERIENCED BY MAVS PIONEER JEFF CLARK IS A THING OF THE PAST. COVER BOY **GRANT "TWIGGY" BAKER,** STILL DOING IT FOR ALL THE RIGHT REASONS.

following spread: SPONSORED GRADE-SCHOOLERS LIKE **CARISSA MOORE** HAVE GROWN UP SURFING THE SORT OF FANTASY WAVES IT ONCE TOOK A SOLID DECADE OF ASCETIC SURF MONK EXISTENCE TO ATTAIN. IT SHOWS IN HER PERFORMANCE.

tape. He wondered out loud if it was smart to show it to me, and I said, "Who am I going to tell?"

Powers's smile said, "Only the whole world, but I still don't know if that's such a good idea."

We found a VCR, and he showed me some scratchy video footage of a warbly big wave somewhere in Northern California. I asked the obvious question, and Tom told me where it was. Aha! No way! That spot we had watched all those years before from Bullet Shell Ridge. Interesting. Guys were riding it now. And they were going right. Good idea. Looking at that initial funky video, I couldn't comprehend how truly monstrous the wave was. And Tom was pretty secretive about it, although he let me know it was a pretty big deal and that Richard Schmidt, Vince Collier, and a lot of the Santa Cruz guys were driving away from giant days at The Lane and Mitchell's Cove and going up there.

I don't remember how much time elapsed between Tom Powers showing me that video at ASR and the next step. Probably I did some phone calling (no e-mail then) and snooping around about what was going on up there. What I found out turned into a pitch for a short "People Who Surf" profile on Half Moon Bay local Jeff Clark, whose name, through the Redwood Wireless, was now being connected with the spot, which by this point had a name: Mavericks. I called Jeff Clark out of the blue, taping our conversation with one of those rotten Radio Shack minicassette recorders that used a suction cup attached to the phone receiver.

By this time, I had been at SURFER a couple of years and was learning the fine arts—one of which was persuading a reluctant surfer to expose a secret he might not want to expose. With someone like Jeff Clark, I first had to present my bona fides: that my dad had lived in Moss Beach since the '70s and had been playing the Sunday gig at the Moss Beach Distillery. I told him about all the gnarly wrecks at the end of Airport Road and pointed out that he probably knew some of the guys who got air and landed in my dad's potted plants.

Clark is monosyllabic until he isn't—ya know? To further work his verbal abalone off the rock, I asked Jeff if that area to the north of Pillar Point was really called Bullet Shell Ridge, explaining my brother's moniker for the place. Turns out that Jeff Clark was a trombone player and the same age as my brother, which meant they had both played in the Half Moon Bay High School marching band under the world famous Phil Macsems. I guess that gave me some pumpkin cred with

Jeff, because he opened up about this spot he had been surfing and protecting for many years.

At some point in the interview, I told Jeff that the decision to expose Mavericks or keep the whole thing quiet was up to him.

"We can open Pandora's box or keep it shut," I said.

"Mavericks will take care of itself," he said.

And that was very true for many years.

SURFER ran that Jeff Clark "People Who Surf" in the December 1991 issue. In it I wrote: "We are daring to breathe the word 'Mavericks' publicly for the first time, only because of the blessing of Jeff Clark." There was an accompanying photo of Jeff surfing Mavericks on a good-size day. It raised a few eyebrows, but the big shock was still to come.

For the June 1992 SURFER magazine, we blew up Mavericks using all the dynamite we had: a cover story, with a three-shot sequence of Pacifica local Darin Bingham riding perhaps the biggest wave yet seen in California. The cover shot was big and blue and almost pleasant-looking, but that was misleading. Steve Hawk's cover blurb promised more inside: California Goes Off.

And I would like to declare here and now that the title of the major feature within that issue came not from me but from Hawk. Perfect titles are a beautiful thing, and "Cold Sweat" was a perfect title. I knew it was good because it made me jealous.

"Cold Sweat" was the big reveal on Mavericks, and to put it simply, the article blew everybody's mind. This was one of the biggest rabbits pulled out of a hat by any surf magazine before or since: a giant wave, as big as Hawaii's fabled Waimea Bay, breaking right off the road in a little Northern California town 25 miles south of San Francisco.

"Cold Sweat" was laid out by Dave Carson, who took his foot off the accelerator a bit and came up with an article that was dark and moody and visually perfect. The opening spread was a pulled-back overview of Jeff Clark from the cliff taken on a gray, ominous, cold afternoon—Christmas Day, in fact. There was also a shot of Steamer Lane hellion Vince Collier at the bottom of a wave that completely filled the frame. And a sequence of Richard Schmidt—who had already made his bones in anything the North Shore could throw at him—wiping out on a wave that was of unimaginable size and ferocity.

The story I wrote still reads well. The facts about the German shepherd for whom the spot was named and Clark surfing it switchfoot, and all alone, for fifteen years, have stood the test of time. There was even a quote from Grant Washburn prophesying that someone would eventually die out there, which famously came true a couple years later. It was probably the most important story I produced during my years at the mag, and in retrospect I probably should have bowed out while I was on top. (Although around 1996 I also dreamed up the Surfer Video Awards, which I am still proud of.)

I stayed at SURFER for many years after that—a Santa Cruz surfer from the '70s not entirely comfortable in southern Orange County in the '90s. Toward the end of the twentieth century, I got shit-canned for punching the head SURFER ad salesman. But it wasn't Ricky Irons Jr. I was punching, it was change: the change that during the '90s came over a sport that seemed altogether too pleased with its rampant commercial growth and the changing role of the surf media, which became increasingly diluted and less special with surf videos, the Internet, and increasing numbers of surf magazines.

I left my watch at SURFER disillusioned. But looking back, I realize that I should be a little jazzed too, because with "Cold Sweat" I did what I had set out to do at SURFER in a bigger way than I ever could have imagined.

Writing about Mavericks paid tribute to Airport Road, my mom and dad, my brothers, the pumpkin festival, and riding motorcycles at Bullet Shell Ridge. I honored all those miles I spent walking from Seventh Avenue to Cowells and back when I was learning, and all those endless hours surfing Pleasure Point, the Hook, the Rivermouth, and the Harbor. By helping to put Mavericks on the map, I paid tribute to the Gallaghers and Leon, Harbor Bill and Tom Hewitt, Mike Locatelli, Wumpy, south swell Shark's Cove, the Johnsons, the O'Neills, and surf movies at the Civic.

I helped give guys like Richard Schmidt, Peter Mel, Flea, and Jay Moriarity a media platform from which they could earn the attention and respect they deserved. But most important, I guess, I got to leave my own mark on surfing's time line, and a writer can't ask for more than that.

WHO WE ARE:

SURFER ON CULTURE

I AM SURFER

above: A YOUNG **BRUCE IRONS** CATCHES UP ON HIS REQUIRED READING.

preceding spread: DURING THE LATE 1970S, NEWPORT BEACH BECAME KNOWN AS "THE HOTTEST HUNDRED YARDS" NOT ONLY FOR THE NEW WAVE ANTICS OF SURFERS LIKE **DANNY KWOCK** (PICTURED HERE) BUT BECAUSE TWO *SURFER* PHOTOGRAPHERS—DAVE EPPERSON AND MIKE MOIR—HAPPENED TO LIVE NEARBY.

WHEN ANIMAL BEHAVIORISTS MEASURE THE INTELLIGENCE QUOTIENT OF A PARTICULAR SPECIES, they use a mirror. If a subject can recognize a reflected image as that of itself, it demonstrates a state of higher awareness generally considered the cornerstone of true intelligence: perception of self. Now while one could produce a number of arguments relating to higher intelligence as it pertains to surfers as a species (board-surfing the Wedge? Rhode Island in winter? Changing in public?), there's no question that since its very first issue, SURFER has been the mirror into which surfers have gazed, searching for self.

This is not to say that surf culture didn't exist long before SURFER premiered in 1960. Those roots had been planted in the early part of the twentieth century by board-riding bohemians like Tom Blake, the father of contemporary surf culture.

"It fits my nature," Blake wrote in his seminal surf tome *Hawaiian Surfriders 1935*, when describing the surfer life. "I can live simply and quietly . . . without the social life. I can dress as I please, for comfort . . . with swimming trunks all day. I can keep one hundred percent suntan . . . rest and sleep for hours in the wonderful sunshine each day."

What, you thought Jeff Spicoli came up with this stuff? The surfer's way has been with us for almost a century, personified by a cast of cultural pioneers who transplanted island style (thanks John Kelly, Wally Froiseth, and George Downing) to the mainland, grafted it to West Coast cool, and kicked off our barefoot adventure, albeit on balsa boards and with no leashes. Pete Peterson, Lorrin Harrison, Dorian Paskowitz,

Burrhead, Dr. Don James, Doc Ball, LeRoy Grannis, Mary Ann Hawkins, Joe Quigg, Tommy Zahn, Buzzy Trent . . . these and many others of less renown made the conscious decision not just to surf but to *be* surfers. That perception of self. But what this earlier generation of surfniks didn't have was the forum that distinguishes a cult, transient by nature, from true culture, defined as " . . . the beliefs, customs, practices, and social behavior of a particular nation or people." The surf movies of the '50s came close, those early screenings attended with the fervor of tent revivals, but again, transient, ephemeral. Nothing a surfer could hold up as proof; no mirror. Not until SURFER.

What surfers look like, what they wear, how they talk, where they surf, how they surf and on what, what they listen to, what they read, what they dream, and how they think: Break the mag down into its basic elements—photography, editorial features, editorial comment, advertisements, and letters from the readers—and you'll find that each of the components contributes to the overall perception of who we are as a culture. In its first few years of publication (remember it started out as a quarterly), SURFER functioned basically as a chronicle—a record of surfing action around the globe. But then the February/March issue of 1962 (the mag having gone bimonthly by then) hinted at a broader aesthetic with a remarkable illustration on its cover. Painted by John Severson himself, it broke from the literal visual reference that SURFER had become and instead used abstract form and color to depict two surfers, tanned to ochre, splayed on an umber beach, their very futuristic surfboards lying askew. (Why surfboard shapers like Dick Brewer and Bob McTavish didn't take the hint from this and other Severson illustrations, which depicted short, pintailed pocket rockets with speed skegs, is one of the sport's great mysteries.) But it was the surfers themselves who sent the message. They were rendered in almost primitive style lying on their backs, the palette's warmth indicating the middle of the day. The deliberate insouciance of the figure with head resting on clasped hands

was Tom Blake's primal vision of the surfer's free and easy life, presented as a piece of religious art for the congregation—at least those with subscriptions or a surf shop nearby—to contemplate. With a few bold strokes, SURFER had transformed from a sporting periodical into an article of faith.

When it comes to tapping into the surfing zeitgeist, has SURFER always been completely in tune? As an editor, Severson, in sharp contrast with his nonrepresentational artistic approach, took a decidedly conservative stance, decrying the antisocial antics of "gremmie hooligans" in favor of the clean-cut sportsmen that began to make regular appearances in the Jantzen ads on the magazine's back cover. And yet the magazine itself featured images of scruffy surfers holed up in North Shore surf shacks, sipping chardonnay on the Côte des Basques, posing before native *rondavals* with bare-breasted Zulu maidens, all for a few waves—and all in the middle of the week. Talk about selling guns to the Indians— who would you rather hang with? Editor Drew Kampion, on the other hand, authentically led the sport into the countercultural conflagration that in the late '60s was sweeping the land. Like some barefoot Bill Graham, Kampion turned SURFER's offices in politically conservative Orange County into an ersatz Fillmore West: the magazine as open mike, promoters and players both reshaping the parameters of self-expression with each radical new performance.

But SURFER could alienate too. Think how much easier it was for editor Steve Pezman, who in the early '70s was dealing with an almost monochromatic culture—didn't we all dress like J-Riddle in the Hang Ten ad: sun-bleached and barefoot, jeans, Hawaiian shirt (or substitute with the screen-print tee), ubiquitous 7'4" winger pin in hand. But as the decades progressed, factions developed—and it's never more obvious than in magazine publication that you can't please all the surfers all the time. Coverage of the burgeoning professional scene in the late '70s outraged the black-neoprened "soul" contingent; "Echo Beach," with its "oh-so-eighties"

polka dots and paint splatters, didn't resemble any beach many SURFER readers called home. The proliferation of purely recreational surfers clogging the lineups with their *fun* boards (the nerve!) in the '90s absolutely mortified Legions of the Truly Obsessed.

It was in the '90s that editor Steve Hawk was dealt perhaps the toughest hand, juggling the magazine's cultural relevance against content that was growing increasingly extreme. The Momentum Generation's high-flying aerial movement represented more than mere tricks— it placed conventional (read: typical) surfers into the role of bystanders, who up to this point could, with a decent cutback or shorebreak tube, at least approximate the surfing of role models like Gerry Lopez and Tom Curren. No longer. Then there was tow-in surfing. It didn't just whip surfers into bigger and bigger waves, but whipped up intense debate as to the essential nature of the act; it challenged what it meant to be a surfer. And Kelly Slater? Who was brave enough to dress like a guy who surfed like that? By the end of the millennium, it was sometimes hard to relate, so rarified had SURFER's reflection become.

And yet even the alienation attested to SURFER's enduring influence on what has developed into a very diverse surf culture: Surfers of every ilk obviously still felt like it was *their* magazine. "How dare you put a longboarder on the cover?" This sort of reader response could only be attributed to a strong sense of self-identification. And today there is more of that in SURFER than at any other time in its history. A flip though the April '09 issue, for example, reveals a two-page spread surfwear ad featuring a Hawaiian waterman, tips on both bodysurfing in a Speedo and pulling a 360 air, a teenage big-wave rider, a fallen pro renouncing substance abuse, a father/ son tuberiding duo, the ASP men and women's top rankings, a surf camp guide, and an article about a college English course being taught on an Indonesian boat trip. After fifty years, there's obviously still plenty of room in this mirror for everyone. —SG

THE SURFER BI-MONTHLY
A John Severson Production
75c
VOL. 3 NO. 3   AUG. – SEPT.
THE INTERNATIONAL SURFING MAGAZINE

MORE OF MURPHY

1 LARRY STRADA, BOB STAY, JOEY CABELL, JUAN SHETRON, AND AN UNIDENTIFIED SUPPORTER CONSIDER THE CULTURAL GULF REPRESENTED BY THE COP'S SHOES. **2** ALLEN SARLO AND RICKY SHAFFER SHARE AN INTIMATE MOMENT WITH A BAND OF THEIR MALIBU BROTHERS. **3** MURPHY, THE ORIGINAL GROM. **4** MIMI MONROE (IN PINK) AND FELLOW FEMALE PIONEERS AT THE 1966 EAST COAST CHAMPIONSHIPS. **5** "HEY, I KNOW THAT DUDE!" SEAN PENN'S DEAD-ON JEFF SPICOLI. **6** MATTY LIU, CUTTING BACK AT THE INTERSECTION OF L.A.'S 405 AND 110 FREEWAYS. **7** MID-'60S FASHION SHOOT. THE BOARDS LOOK RIGHT, BUT DID GIRLS REALLY STAND LIKE THAT? **8** JOHN MCCLURE, DOGTOWN, '80S-STYLE. **9** THE DORA LEGEND LIVES.

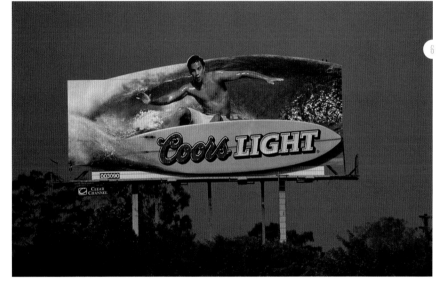

❶ IN 2010 RESIN-STAINED ARTISANS ASSURED THAT THE TERM "SURFBOARD INDUSTRY" WAS STILL AN OXYMORON. ❷ FORMER RIVALS AND CURRENTLY THE SPORT'S MOST SUCCESSFUL TOW-IN TEAM, **MIKE PARSONS** AND **BRAD GERLACH**. ❸ GROMS RULE—AT LEAST THEY DID AT OTHER SURF MAGAZINES' MARKETING EVENTS. ❹ OAHU'S NORTH SHORE, WHERE MEN ARE MEN AND SO ARE THE BOYS. ❺ **PARKER COFFIN,** NOT ALL THT BROKEN UP.

following spread: NEW FACE IN AN OLD SCENE: **KASSIA MEADOR** PERSONIFIES THE TWENTY-FIRST-CENTURY SURFER, RIDING WHAT SHE WANTS, HOW SHE WANTS, WHERE SHE WANTS.

EDITING *SURFER:* THE ULTIMATE REALITY

BY DREW KAMPION

"WE RIDE THE SEA THIS WAY,
OUR OWN PECULIAR SEA
THAT MAKES ITS WAVES
IN THIS DARK STATIC AT THE FRINGE OF
THE UNIVERSAL CONSCIOUSNESS;
THE WAVES, TOO, ECHOES OF POWER
AS WE ALL ARE ECHOES OF SOME POWER
AND BROTHERS BY OUR
VERY DIMINUTIVE PRESENCE
TOGETHER ON THE PERIPHERY
OF GOD'S EXPLODED MEMORY."

DREW KAMPION
SURFER (VOL. 11, NO. 2, MAY 1970)

Normally, objects get smaller as they get farther away. Events, not necessarily so. Through the lens of history and hindsight, things tend to warp weirdly, sometimes growing larger in the distance and even assuming new shapes. My time at SURFER was short, but looking back on it now, I see that it changed everything in my life and perhaps also changed some things in the surfing world.

Through an odd conjunction of circumstances and events, I found myself in the role of associate editor of SURFER in June of 1968. John Severson had invited me down from Santa Cruz to attend that year's Surfer Poll, where he offered me the job based on a trio of stories I had written for the magazine. Within a month, I had replaced Pat McNulty as editor, with John as my mentor.

During the early 1960s, with no prior publishing experience himself, John had figured out how to put together a magazine. By the time I arrived, everything about his system and process was orderly, professional, and inspired. But for me, new to the magazine business, the SURFER office was a creative laboratory. On a strict regimen of ten joints and twenty cups of coffee a day, I could write, edit, work on layouts, pick through photos, doodle, take pictures, talk on the phone long-distance, take a surf break, whatever. It was the best kind of school.

The schedule was nice too—bimonthly, which created an excellent lifestyle pace: a month to travel, surf, take care of business, and experience the world, and a month to build a magazine. It was just right for the small staff: Shirley at the front desk, Larry Rink and then Hy Moore in the art department, Brad Barrett in the photo department (when he wasn't out shooting a contest or an ad photo), John's dad Hugh in accounting, Don Thomas and the late, great Don Kremers selling ads, John working on his golf game and his film, and the magazine—just enough to guide me, really. I was pretty much free to do whatever I wanted to do, which is why those issues from '68 to '71 had so much of my own self-indulgence in them. Apparently, I was having a little too much fun.

Prior to becoming editor, I didn't know any big-name surfers. I had met Bob Cooper and John Peck in Ventura and at Rincon, and I had been snaked by Dora and Dewey and Fain at Malibu, but when it came to surf-celebrity culture, I was pretty much clueless. My introduction to the celebrity surfing world had been that 1968 Poll banquet at the San Clemente Inn, and now I was apparently at its hub—I joined John for lunch with Hobie and Phil Edwards, I surfed Trestles with Chuck Dent and Steve Bigler. The SURFER office was a nexus for drop-ins by contemporary and future legends, from seminal surf-traveler Peter Troy to contest prodigy Corky Carroll to mild-mannered insurgent Mickey Muñoz. Ron Stoner drifted in and out. Rick Griffin came by occasionally. Even Dora visited a couple of times.

We at SURFER were part of a major paradigm shift, a full-on countercultural coup attempt. The Man was the enemy. Vietnam and the draft were the major issues of the day, and surfers were either avoiding it or had been caught up in it. The beach was quieter for the absence of thousands of alpha males; peace and love ruled the lineups, mostly.

At the height of all this, in the summer of '69, Nixon moved into the house next door to the Seversons. Any time he was in residence, we were barred from the beach south of the "Western White House" property line, which meant Cottons, Trestles, and Church. Meanwhile, heads of state from around the world were parading through John's neighborhood, along with Tricky Dick's entire Washington posse. This (and the fact that our phones were all tapped) really provoked a mood of rebellion among the SURFER staff, and subjects like offshore oil-drilling (and the Santa Barbara Channel spill of '69), proposed harbors, loss of beach access, development-related pollution, and related issues translated into an increasingly activist editorial stance. The casual writing around these topics later crystallized into a section of the magazine called "Our Mother Ocean"—a voice for nascent ecological advocacy.

Nixon, Vietnam, and the emerging environmental consciousness were just part of the picture. The surfing world itself had been shocked by a new approach to riding waves predicated on the use of drastically smaller vehicles. The surfboard industry had been brought to its knees by the burden of enormous inventories of huge boards when customers suddenly demanded half-size craft. At the same time, because the overall mood of the times was essentially anti-establishment, the big brands found themselves marginalized and threatened with irrelevance as hardcore surfers migrated to local garage shops for their sticks. A new generation of surfer-shapers was translating its understanding of "what was happening" into exciting and revolutionary vehicles. The story of the shortboard revolution and the emergence of the economy of underground shapers was heralded and chronicled (and some would say advanced) in the pages of SURFER.

DREW KAMPION

Alongside stories about equipment, articles in SURFER addressed the essential nature of surfing. Is competition a good thing, or is it actually a self-evidently stupid thing? In other words, is surfing a sport or is it an art? Or is it, as Nat Young stated, a religion? Competitive surfing, so popular in the mid-'60s, reached its nadir in the early '70s, and the no-logo, black-wetsuit ethos has remained in vogue in surfing's most "organic" enclaves to this day.

An oxymoronic "back to the land" movement appeared within surfing, as it did in the culture at large, doubtless propelled by an urgency to leave humanity's current insanity far behind. The momentum of war and shades of police-state repression were balanced with an urgency to explore more personal realms. An atmosphere of experimentation, spontaneity, and permissiveness prevailed.

I think those were the very best years to be the editor of SURFER. The cosmic egg cracked open, and I fell through. I landed in a world peopled with an extraordinary tribe of individuals: surfers, certainly—George Downing, Wally Froiseth, Nat, Midget, Dent, Martinson, Bigler, Noll, Crump, Hakman, Cabell, Doyle, Greenough, Wayne Lynch, Corky, David, Skip, BB, Hemmings, Reno, Rolf, Fain and Dora, Peck, Butch, Buzzy, Barry K, Skip, Freddie and Randy, the Van Dykes, Ricky Grigg—but artists, too, especially Spider Wills, Greg MacGillivray, Sevo, Bruce Brown, the Witzigs, Art Brewer, Ed Schumpert, John Van Hamersveld, Stern, and Bill Cleary.

In August of 1970, just twenty-six months after I had arrived, I pulled up stakes and moved back to Santa Cruz, becoming an editor "at large" for the magazine, which is to say a freelance writer. One of my most enjoyable writing experiences at the magazine followed almost immediately. I wrote a quirky, dystopian, witty little piece titled "Creature from the Green Room," which was illustrated by John Severson. That remains my favorite collaboration with the man who invented the surf magazine.

So, my editorship was a short tour of duty: Dana Point, San Clemente, Puerto Rico, Australia, and Hawaii. Plus, I had a couple great trips to the Ranch (recalling Motorskil and those *Pacific Vibrations*) and a few runs to Baja. I had the chance to sit down face-to-face with many (perhaps most) of the great surfing talents of the day.

Certainly these experiences expanded my world. The influence I had on SURFER and the larger surfing world was largely because I came to the role of editor with few preconceptions and with so little connection to any established hierarchy. I tended to be open to virtually any subject, author, or approach. As it happened, I continued on the twin paths of writing and surfing. Somehow they've had a resonant compatibility for me. Surfing is the ultimate metaphor . . . and the ultimate reality.

opposite: SURFER ART DIRECTOR LARRY RINK'S PSYCHEDELIC DAY-GLO COVER OF
ROGER ADAMS, MARCH 1968.

above: SURFER ACTUALLY HELPED PERPETUATE THE DIVISIVE ETHIC OF LOCALISM
BY SIMPLY DEPICTING IT. SUNSET CLIFFS, EARLY '70S.

"THE SIMPLE MESSAGE OF THIS EDITORIAL IS THAT OBNOXIOUS BEHAVIOR, SEEDY APPEARANCE OR BADGES AND SYMBOLS DON'T MAKE THE SURFER. BY HIS FELLOW SURFER HE MAY BE LAUGHED AT OR LOOKED DOWN UPON, WHILE AT THE SAME TIME HE IS CREATING A BAD IMAGE IN THE EYES OF THE PUBLIC. DON'T BE A BADGE WEARER— BE A SURFER."

JOHN SEVERSON
FROM "THE SIGN OF THE KOOK," AUGUST/SEPTEMBER 1963

WHY GIRLS?

A girl appeared in the very first issue of SURFER: fifteen-year-old Linda Benson, flying through the shorebreak at Makaha. A female surfer first appeared on a SURFER cover in September 1964, followed by Linda Merrill on the cover of the very next issue. The Surfer Poll has included women since 1964 (won that year and the following three years by Joyce Hoffman). The March 1966 issue featured a shot of a French surfer posed on the beach with her board. Margo Oberg was featured on the cover in May 1981, and she was followed two issues later by the July "Women of the Sea" cover story. There were the "Lisa Andersen Surfs Better Than You" cover in September 1996 and the "Carissa Moore Surfs Better Than You" cover in May 2009. So what? So women haven't been completely shut out of SURFER throughout the years. Not completely . . . but close. In 1964's uncredited "Why Girls" feature SURFER concluded: ". . . they have an equal right to ride waves along with all surfers. But remember girls—you also have equal rights to carry your own boards, swim in after a wipeout, and no special privileges on the waves!" Not exactly encouraging. And granted, until very recently, the overall percentage of female surfers in the water has been very low. During the late '70s and early '80s for example, female surfers were so rare that the women's pro tour was virtually the only place you'd see more than three of them together at the same time. SURFER has to shoulder some of the blame for this cultural snubbing—had the magazine presented women surfers integrally, rather than as an anomaly, we might not have had to wait so long for the Roxy Girl to appear in the marketing campaign that became a movement. But once she did show up in her girl trunks and a smile, SURFER got right on the message: A woman's place isn't only on the pro tour but also at any beach, in any surf, out there simply having fun. ▬

WE'RE ALL LOCALS

By 1973 it had all changed: Only ten short years separated "Surfin' USA" from "Locals Only!" And if **SURFER** helped perpetuate this new exclusionary ethic with its use of surf-spot pseudonym—most conspicuously in regard to certain breaks in San Diego and Ventura Counties—along with the collective White Man's Guilt that colored much of its coverage of Hawaiian territorialism, it did so with obvious reluctance. As was evidenced by a 1974 SURFER "Extra," in which the letter reprinted below was run with an uncaptioned photo of two surfers fighting, the simple headline *A Poignant Plea for Sanity*, its message as relevant today as it was thirty-five years ago:

Surfing has always been a way of life for me. The fondest memories I have are of my days in the tubes with my surfing brothers. Sitting up on a cold winter night, it seems so far away. Memories—the first time I got tubed. Whoosh! Unreal. The one and only 10-foot day I ever saw. Seeing Five Summer Stories *and being unbelievably stoked by it all. My first contest, parties and chicks and the whole outrageous gig. I remember hearing ugly rumors about Sebastian and Cocoa beach locals. When I got there I found them to be unreal people. I guess every surfer really is your brother if you treat him as such. I punched out a guy at Threes last year. If he's reading this, I'd like to say I'm sorry . . . throughout my life I have come to love these people and, more importantly, the ocean that we all lived for. I was going to graduate high school in June. I had saved enough money to go to the North Shore next year. I thought I was ready but the doctor says no. See, I'm 17 and I got cancer. Yeah, I'm dying. I'll lie here in a hospital bed and when the summer swell starts pumping, I'll be dead. Geez, I only wrote this so you people would realize how lucky you are; to be able to live this life is a privilege I'll never have again. For your own good, cut out the hassles. Surfing shouldn't be a rip off, it should be a beautiful art, an affair with the sea that I'll miss more than anything . . . except Fran.* ▬

preceding spread: THE '60S WEREN'T ALL ABOUT REVOLUTION. RICHARD CHEW, ABOUT AS STRAIGHT AS YOU CAN GET AND STILL BAREFOOT.

opposite: LISA ANDERSEN, SURFING LIKE A GIRL.

below: FIGHTING FOR WAVES.

SURFER CROSS

In 1966's "The Sign of the Kook," contributing editor Bill Cleary conducted a not-so-very objective interview with renowned art designer Ed "Big Daddy" Roth, originator of the "Rat Fink," "Surf-ink," and the ubiquitous "Surfer's Cross." More of an interrogation than question-and-answer, Cleary charged Roth with misrepresenting, albeit graphically, "real" surfers who wanted nothing to do with the symbolism associated with the German Maltese cross.

"The cross itself has not hurt the sport," explained Roth. "For anyone who's not hip to what's happening I want to say that these surfers who wear the cross are not neo-Nazis."

"Very commendable," quipped Cleary. "But are you really so sure they're surfers in the first place?"

"Sure," says Roth. "We see the surfers everwhere—in Denver . . . Chicago. Wherever we go we see surfers. They may not be able to surf, but they act and dress like surfers . . ."

"That's the crux of the matter," replies Cleary.

And has remained the crux ever since. Just how do you maintain the authenticity—the intimacy—that is essential to the magazine's core audience, while at the same time encouraging the sport (and the publication) to grow and prosper? It's true that throughout the decades SURFER's fortunes have ebbed and flowed with the tide of mainstream infatuation—several waves of skateboard advertisements and Midwest-manufactured surfwear companies have crested and crashed between its covers. But at its heart SURFER has always expressed a very strong sense of "us and them," its primary doctrine being aimed directly at the faithful.

"I see the question not as 'What do you surf?' or 'Where do you surf?'" wrote editor in chief Joel Patterson in a 2009 editorial, "as much as 'Why do you surf?' And the beauty of that question is that there are literally no wrong answers. So long as you actually *do* surf." ▬

JUKEBOX HEROES

What is it with modern surf stars and guitars? Three decades of SURFER passed with few, if any, musical surf savants. Sure, in the '60s Danny Brawner, Hobie's top laminator, played drums for The Sandals on the classic *Endless Summer* theme. The '70s saw U.S. Champ Corky Carroll attempt a troubadour's career, only to get repeatedly gonged. And in the '80s, Tom Curren's considerable musical abilities were completely overshadowed by his amazing surfing performances—an arrangement that suited the reclusive world champ just fine, his singing and songwriting a much more personal form of self-expression than, say, tuberiding Off-the-Wall. Yet by the mid-'90s it seemed that just about every up-and-comer had picked up a guitar and had endeavored to strike the same chord: surfer as rock star. Oh, it wasn't a new concept. SURFER's 1974 Photo Annual featured a shot of two imperious Hawaiian hotshots hanging at Rocky Point, captioned "Rock stars Reno Abellira and Jimmy Lucas. . . ." The term "surf star," which first appeared in the pages of SURFER that same year, was simply a derivative of the term. But it wasn't until modern times that the two archetypes actually merged—and no, we don't mean "Songs from The Pipe" by The Surfers (featuring Kelly Slater, Peter King, and Rob Machado) or any performances alongside ardent surf groupie and former Pearl Jam front man Eddie Vedder (who hasn't been up onstage with him?) This leaves us with a swelling new wave of surf-musicians, from the relatively obscure (Andrew Kidman and his Val Dusty Experiment, Alex Knost and The Japanese Motors) to the ubiquitous Donavon Frankenreiter, who over the course of several albums has actually enjoyed some Top 40 and commercial success. Then there's Timmy Curran, who segued from the ASP Tour to a concert tour with very little warning, and, of course, Jack Johnson, the monster of all hot surfers-turned-sensitive-singer-songwriters. All of them playing the guitar—not a drum or bass or tambourine among them. ▬

opposite: SURFERS? NOT WITH THOSE HAIRY ARMS AND MALTESE CROSSES.

above: DONAVON FRANKENREITER ON LEAD, WITH *SURFER'S* MATT GEORGE (LEFT) ON BACKUP.

THE REAL THING

It's the oldest latest concept in surfing history: the artificial wave.

In the May 1965 issue, a SURFER editorial by Patrick McNulty posed the question: "Wave Machine—A Reality?"

"The day may be fast approaching when the need for artificial spots becomes a reality," opined McNulty. "What would happen if a surf-making machine went on sale today?"

The funny thing is, SURFER has been answering that question for more than forty-five years, with scores of articles concerning artificial reefs and wave pools, from coverage of Japan's first "Surf-a-Torium" wave pool (January 1967) and the opening of Big Surf in Tempe, Arizona (September 1968) to coverage of 1985's World Professional Inland Surfing Championships held at the Dorney Park & Wildwater Kingdom in Allentown, Pennsylvania, occasional free-surf days at Typhoon Lagoon in Florida's Disney World, and the exotic Sunway Bandar Wavepool in Kuala Lumpur, Malaysia. The more organic alternative has also seen plenty of press, from 1969's "Artificial Reef" feature by renowned surfer/oceanographer Rick Grigg to continuing coverage of the failed "Pratte's Reef" project in El Segundo (2000). And in the April 2004 issue, SURFER offered a full-blown examination of the topic titled "Man vs. Nature," in which editor in chief Sam George contrasted the inadvertent creation of waves with the ongoing dream of "man-made" tubes.

" . . . the coastlines of the world are littered with breaks that without man's helping hand—man's uncaring and often destructive hand—otherwise would not exist," wrote George. "His piers, jetties, channels, groins, breakwalls, and dredge-tailing sandbars have come to define some of surfing's most traditional landscapes, providing as merely an engineering byproduct waves that in many cases rival the best nature itself has to offer."

The first "man-made" wave appeared on the cover of SURFER in June 1964 (Ala Moana), the very latest in January of 2009 (Lighthouse Jetties, Cape Hatteras), illustrating the fact that while we obviously love pondering the question of "artificial" waves, we've been riding them all along. ▬

THE EMBASSY

BY BERNIE BAKER

BERNIE BAKER

The classic island cottage at Sunset Beach that became my home was just that—the first house built on the sand there in the 1930s. It was surfer/shaper Ryan Dotson and his girlfriend's digs when I first moved over from Carpenteria, California, by way of Maui, in 1972. After they'd moved on, a friend of Ryan's bunked there for a couple seasons, after which I was somehow handed the keys—the simple turn of fate that led to my tenure at "The Embassy" at Sunset Beach.

That first month cost me a used lawn mower, $150 security, and the $150 month's rent—plus I had to keep the grass mowed for the Wilkinson family from Kailua, who owned the clapboard one-bedroom beach house. It was originally set up as a summer getaway for the Wilkinson's grandparents, which explains the expansive back porch—the lanai—that faced straight out onto the Sunset Beach lineup. For this same reason, it almost immediately became a gathering place for surfers, photographers, and hangers-on. Sunset Beach in the early '70s was the main North Shore arena.

The house was small, but it sat on a big grassy lot so big that we'd set up a volleyball court in summer, and during the winter surf season I'd even let a few cars park on it. My Camaro (and *Island Style* photography partner Leonard Brady's Corvette) hogged most of the driveway.

Kenny Bradshaw always walked over from his shack down the beach by Kammieland. In those days the lifeguard tower was located at our end of the beach, just a few yards away from the house, and guards like Butch Akauka, Darrick Doerner, and the guys left all their gear under the house next to the outside shower. I'd built it with a forty-gallon tank so there was plenty of hot water to go around after those late-afternoon sessions. And I needed plenty too. The Embassy (I think it was the late Mark Foo who gave it its official moniker) turned out to be the main rescue station for Sunset—I can't count how many boards we saved from the rip on the big days. In those preleash days, a wipeout would mean swimming in, running up into the yard, grabbing the binos off the lanai, and searching the channel for the loose gun being swept out to sea in the current. Didn't matter what color it was (red was best), you still needed to get up on high ground to scan the rip for the board . . . and then you had to race back down, run the beach, dive into the channel, and start swimming your ass off to get to it some quarter mile offshore. A lot of fun at twilight, and chilly work too, with the trades blowing down off Paumalu.

I never locked that house up when I was gone— there were always too many friends hanging around the yard, checking the surf, or scanning the beach for girls. On those flat sunny days you could count on Foo spending more time on the lanai than anyone, maintaining his top position for beach chick-counting.

On the good winter days, it was just first-come for parking, and it was nuts. No one wanted to park on the Kam Highway with extra boards in his car, so if there was no alternative but to park on the street, you'd often find twenty quivers of guns stacked up all over the yard. Everyone had their stash in their own "personal zone" including food, towels, clothes, and wallets. The unspoken rule was that anything you brought into the yard was safe, and I was amazed that even Sunset's ordinarily light-fingered parking-lot crew respected the boundaries.

Status at Sunset didn't just apply in the lineup. Mark Richards would race in with this older-model BMW (that he bought from an ex-girlfriend-for-a-season) as early as he could so it could sit next to the Camaro and the 'Vette. To this day I have no idea how he thought his Eurotrash ride had any image-sharing qualities with American iron, but he did, so we just humored him with a parking slot behind ours. Meanwhile Lightning Bolt's Jack Shipley had

this full-blown Ranchero with a Hurst shifter, and it was all engine up front, so the horsepower lineup was equal to the Tom Parrish gun stash in the yard and under the house. Then there was local boy Vince Klyn, to whom we once sold one of our used VWs. Thing was Vince told us that he was sixteen—legal driving age in Hawaii—when he was really only fourteen. So he would hide the Vee-Dub in the bushes by my house at night, get a ride home, and then hitch back out and proudly drive it around the North Shore during the day.

In time, and with the world of professional surfing growing each year, the little house on the beach became a real embassy. Rabbit, Shaun and Michael Tomson, Mark Warren, Bruce Raymond, Reno Abellira (a.k.a. King Farouk), Rory, Bobby Owens, Jeff Divine, Harry Hodge, Steve Jones, Mark Foo, Kenny Bradshaw, Mark Richards: Surfers from all over the world, with or without girlfriends, spent so many of their days in that yard or on my deck, hanging in the shade. Sometimes it was as much a political refuge as it was a hangout. I can't count how many times a visiting surfer would paddle in quickly and walk across the beach and up through my yard to the highway so that whatever seriously pissed-off local couldn't find him. Maybe even once or twice I'd tell the unfortunate "drop-in" to go inside and watch TV, then act dumb to whoever was right on his tail, looking for blood.

The Wilkinsons eventually sold the property— it's now a huge, opulent vacation rental, and I'm pretty sure nobody parks on the lawn anymore. But for me it will always be the beach house, and ten years of the greatest show on Earth at one of the greatest locations in the world. I wouldn't trade those memories for love or money, or anything else that might have made me miss out on all the epic surf, social insanity, and the best friends I've ever known.

following spread: BERNIE'S PORCH. CAN YOU SPOT PAUL NAUDE, CHRIS FULSTON, LARRY BLAIR, SIMON ANDERSON, HARRY HODGE, JEFF HAKMAN, PHIL BYRNE, SHAUN TOMSON, PETER DROUYN, AND TERRY FITZGERALD?

WORST 5 LOOKS

1. **THE 2-INCH-INSEAM SHORTS.** APPARENTLY NOBODY HAD ANY BALLS IN THE EARLY 1980s—AND WE MEAN THAT LITERALLY. WHAT ELSE COULD EXPLAIN THE PROLIFERATION OF SURF TRUNKS AND WALKING SHORTS THAT, WHILE THEY MAY HAVE LEFT A LITTLE ROOM FOR IMAGINATION, ACCOMMODATED VERY LITTLE ELSE—AT LEAST IN THE CROTCH DEPARTMENT.

2. **DAY-GLO HOME.** IN THE MID-1960s, SURFER ART DIRECTOR JOHN VAN HAMERSVELD'S CLASSIC ENDLESS SUMMER POSTER PIONEERED THE USE OF DAY-GLO. BUT IT SHOULD NEVER HAVE BEEN APPLIED TO FASHION, ESPECIALLY ELASTIC-WAIST VOLLEY-SHORTS THAT MADE EVEN THE BEST SURFERS LOOK LIKE SISSIES.

3. **TIE-DIE.** SURFERS WERE THE ORIGINAL FUNCTION-OVER-FASHION BRIGADE—THE SURF TRUNK AND SCREEN-PRINT T-SHIRT ARE EXCEPTIONAL EXAMPLES OF EFFICIENCY AND ELOQUENCE. SO, NOTHING IS WORSE THAN SURFERS DRESSING LIKE PARTICIPANTS IN OTHER SUBCULTURES: IN THIS CASE, AN EARLY '70s TIE-DYED-LEVI'S-WITH-NO-SHIRT HIPPIE LOOK. AND THE ONLY THING MORE MISERABLE THAN WET JEANS IS THE SMELL OF PATCHOULI.

4. **THE SURFER "LOOK."** ALL THEY HAD TO DO IS FLIP THROUGH THE PAGES OF SURFER TO SEE WHAT SURFERS DRESSED LIKE. YET AS FAR BACK AS THE EARLY '60s, LABELS LIKE CATALINA SEEMED CONVINCED THAT SURFERS ACTUALLY WORE MATCHING TRUNKS AND WINDBREAKERS, PERPETUATING A SURFER "LOOK" THAT LOOKED NOTHING LIKE A REAL SURFER.

5. **STICKER SHOCK.** PRO SURFING HAS CONTRIBUTED MANY WONDERFUL THINGS TO OUR CULTURE: THE PIPE MASTERS, THE THRUSTER . . . THE THRUSTER. BUT BEGINNING IN THE LATE '70s, ONE OF ITS MOST DUBIOUS INNOVATIONS HAS BEEN THE WIDESPREAD POPULARITY OF THE STICKER. TODAY IT'S HARD TO EVEN IMAGINE A SURF WORLD WITHOUT ADHESIVES, YET THERE WAS A TIME WHEN SURFBOARDS WERE PAINTED, LOGOS WERE INDELIBLE, BOTTOMS WERE CLEAN, AND WAX WAS DIRTY.

First Team Off Shore is the special commitment to quality in active wear. Designed by water people as the ultimate garment in fashion and quality, the metalite surf trunk can only be found at select surf shops across the country.

The competitive attitude that insures high fashion and quality is symbolized by the rising sun of First Team Off Shore.

OFF SHORE FIRST TEAM: LARRY BLAIR, MIKE BENAVIDEZ, MICHAEL HO AND CHRIS BARELA.

METALITE

OFF SHORE SPORTSWEAR FOR MEN AND WOMEN · 3221 W. MacARTHUR BLVD., SANTA ANA, CA 92704 · 714/751-6322

HAWAII 808/395-3982 · TOKYO/JAPAN 03-793-7626 · ACCESSORIES 714/832-5500 · SANDALS 714/549-2032 · SCREEN PRINTS 408/263-7007

Catalina SURFERS® made of Nylon by Chariot Textiles Corp., are quick-drying, rugged and durable. Here Catalina's "Wave Blazer" Pullover, $7.95 and "Wave Blazer" Surf Trunk, $5.95. When you think of authentic SURFERS®, Think Catalina first!

Fabric by

Chariot Textiles Corp.

Norane-W *Durable* WATER REPELLENT
505 EIGHTH AVENUE, NEW YORK 18, N. Y. OXford 5-0625

SURFER® IS A REGISTERED TRADEMARK OF CATALINA INC.

BEING A CORRESPONDENT FOR SURFER

BY JOHN WITZIG

above: **JOHN WITZIG**

following spread: ILLUSTRATOR **PHIL ROBERTS** PRODUCED
A NUMBER OF GROUNDBREAKING IMAGES FOR *SURFER*
OVER THE YEARS, INCLUDING A SERIES OF SURF
SPOT LINEUPS, SEVERAL COVERS, AND HIS HUGELY
ENTERTAINING PORTRAITS OF PERIOD PRO SCENES.

SOMEWHERE I HAVE A *SURFER* BUSINESS CARD WITH MY NAME ON IT.

Somewhere I have a SURFER business card
with my name on it. I'm not sure just when
they gave it to me, but possibly it was when I
was in California to do a story that ended up
being a three-part piece published in 1981. I was
very impressed by the card, but I'm not sure I
showed it to many people—my vanity was at
least partially offset by the fear of being seen
as a show-off. Simply *saying* you were writing a
story for the magazine was a pretty good entrée
to just about any place and anyone in the surfing
world—at that time anyway.

It's just about impossible to overemphasize the impact that the first issue of SURFER had on me in Australia in 1960. It was around the time I saw my first balsa surfboard, and Bud Browne's early films were being toured. *All* of it was revelatory, but maybe nothing more so than the magazine. I was sixteen years old and already a bit publication-obsessive. I doubt that the possibility of being involved occurred to me, but the fact that surfing magazines *existed* was enough to excite my imagination.

The first Australian surfing magazines arrived a year or two later. Spurred on by a youthful mix of arrogance and certainty, I contributed my first story to *Surfing World* in 1963 and designed and edited my first issue of the magazine in mid-1966. This experience led pretty much directly to submitting a story to SURFER that hadn't attracted any attention at all when it had been published in Australia a few months previously. This was the piece that John Severson titled "We're Tops Now." That unfortunate title and a couple of minor editorial changes managed to make my already florid prose even *more* extravagant, and it caused something of a stir. Nick Carroll (who wasn't altogether averse to hyperbole) would much later describe the piece as "splendidly inflammatory."

It was evidently in the hope that I'd repeat my youthful indiscretions that I was invited to review the state of surfing in California in mid-1980. Jim Kempton was the editor and Steve Pezman the publisher. Kempton didn't like me, and the antipathy was mutual, but he understood the value of controversy, and my writing had the potential to draw a lot of readership.

I had a terrific month in California, spent *everything* (and then some) I was being paid for the story, was self indulgent—the opportunities were endless—and managed to come up with the piece that was run in 1981. More than two decades later, I still believe it was entertaining and not without a bit of insight.

The advantages I had as the Australian abroad were several: I was *far* less polite than most Americans, and so more capable of causing offence should it be necessary (and I would not be around to face the consequences); I was *way* more skeptical, and less respectful, of anything and everything that I happened across than any local could possibly be; and I also genuinely *liked* the many and diverse Californians that I met and, as far as I could see at that time, not too many members of any one crew liked too many members of another crew much at all.

SURFER was *always* prudish about using words like *fuck* (and I have a dirty mouth), so some self-censorship was required. They actually even changed the word *dick* to *organ* in "the smaller the board, the smaller the dick" that I quoted in the first part of the California trilogy. I mean, I got used to it (what else was there to do?) and found it almost (though not quite) endearing in a way. Australian surfing publications (well, since *Tracks* anyway) have always been less conservative and more (refreshingly?) vulgar. Maybe each is just mirroring its community, but from what I know of the two communities, I'm not sure about that.

As a postscript of sorts, I again suffered the slings and arrows of outrageous editing. *Somehow*, my reference to the (respected) views of (Drew) "Kampion" became "Kempton" in the published text. This was *surely* a proofing error rather than rank self-aggrandizement. It provoked me to pen a vicious (and probably defamatory) letter to the editor that, fortunately, I never sent. But I showed it, with some amusement, to then-editor Chris Mauro just before the story was included in the anthology of writings from SURFER that was published in 2007, and, finally, a correction was made.

If my relationships with various editors have been sometimes fractious—Drew Kampion being the singular exception—I've mostly got on better with the photography department. I treasure an e-mail from Jeff Divine titled "Look what I found." Attached was a scan of a transparency of Nat in Hawaii in 1967 with the V-bottom board that, a very short time later, would lead surfing performance into more vertical lines. I'd managed to lose track of that (and too many other) significant pictures, and the SURFER archive has saved my bacon on a number of occasions.

The photography editor *always* had the editor to blame for picture choices I've disagreed with. The editor has nowhere to hide when he's made a cut I've thought merely injudicious or *really* stupid. In my limited experience, the photography department also has had a more fun-loving attitude to recreational activities.

There were some low points. I incurred the wrath of whoever was the editor at the time when I submitted a bill for a lunch that Peter Crawford and I had to relieve the boredom while we were doing a story on Sydney. It wasn't so much the total amount of the bill that caused the problem, it was the fact that the wine component was higher than the food. The fact that this seemed quite reasonable to me only magnified the perceived abuse.

I burned another bridge when the pictures I'd been paid to shoot at the World Championships in Victoria in 1970 turned out to be mostly overexposed and pretty well useless. That wasn't my finest hour.

But there were also high points—I didn't at all mind the infamy of "We're Tops Now," and the magazine obviously reveled in it; I liked a small piece called "The View at Beacon" that I wrote while staying in Encinitas in 1976; and the overview of the winter on the North Shore that year stands up pretty well too.

Writing for SURFER during the period that I did was mainly a mix of fun and self-gratification, with a modicum of apparent prestige (the business card) thrown in—the flattery was required to compensate for the none-too-abundant editorial payments. Fortunately (or unfortunately) I've never lost the buzz of first opening a magazine I've contributed to. That's a *really* nice thing to do.

WHAT WE SEE:
SURFER ON PHOTOGRAPHY

BEHIND THE LENS

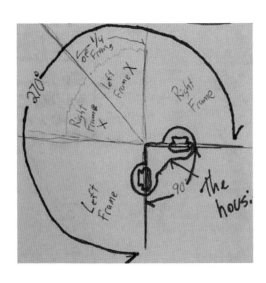

IN 2007, CONTRIBUTING *SURFER* PHOTOGRA-PHER SCOTT AICHNER submitted an extraordinary collection of images—and this from a man who over the past decade has made amazing photographs his trademark. Aichner specializes in water photography—and more specifically the use of a waterproof, wide-angle lens requiring the photographer to swim into the hollow heart of the wave, literally inches from his surfing subjects. His affable nature on land belies a fearless determination to capture the most intimate perspectives on the surfing act. Regularly kicking out into some of the world's most fearsome lineups, pistol-grip water housing held high, Aichner redefined the term "action photography" by placing himself deeper in the curl than the surfers themselves; if Aichner had been a wartime photojournalist he'd have been shooting from the middle of no man's land, shells exploding all round him. But his 2007 submission astounded even those SURFER editors who'd almost grown used to what were now deemed "Aichner Shots." Having developed a revolutionary 180-degree, two-camera water housing, the intrepid Aichner had been positioning himself inside the wave to simultaneously record twin perspectives in a single photo: one looking into the tube at the surfer racing for daylight, and the second from the surfer's point of view looking out of the curl from deep within the wave. The results were spectacular,

regardless of the sport Aichner had focused on—the view both up and down the course during a downhill-ski race, for example. But what makes Aichner's breakthrough photography more remarkable is what's not in the images. Put simply, Aichner regularly works in a space that doesn't exist. The breaking wave, a fleeting pulse of energy rippling through a liquid medium, appears only once and then vanishes without a trace, the tube formed within the wave essentially a transient space in time, ever moving forward, never being. The essence of surf photography has been to capture that most ephemeral of moments; from the first grainy Surf Fever frame grabs that filled the premier issue, the essence of SURFER has always been its photography.

Surfers have long been fascinated with their own image, and more specifically an image they could hold in their hands. The 1950s surf films mesmerized their early audiences, but there was something insubstantial about the film experience. The movies were too much like the waves themselves—appearing briefly, thrilling mightily, and then disappearing—leaving the surfer in a constant state of conjecture. Surfers may have loved surf movies, but they needed surf photos. SURFER gave them photos. In fact, John Severson began his career as a publisher selling black-and-white eight-by-ten surf prints at his film screenings. Once the magazine began regular publication, the role of still photography in the development and expansion of the sport became paramount: the big waves of the North Shore; surfing up, down, and around U.S. coastlines; longboard style; shortboard revolution; wild waves from Makaha to the Mentawais; low rails and high aerials; surf stars from LJ to CJ, from Dane to Dane, Curren to Kelly—a pictorial time line of the sport functioning both as reference point and inspiration for more than five decades.

SURFER's roster of photo editors and contributing photographers past and present is a literal who's who. John Severson, who perfected follow-focus techniques with the Century 1000 lens, was the magazine's primary eye in the early days and, though often uncredited, produced many of the most iconic images. The methodical Ron Church introduced contemporary photojournalism with his moody black-and-whites, while all-around waterman and innovator Bev Morgan provided the sort of immersive water shots that in the years afterward would become SURFER's staple. Then there was the mercurial Ron Stoner, whose perception of composition and color defined the period from 1964 to 1967, widely considered "The Longboard Era." There were other surf photographers around in the mid-'60s, but none with Stoner's sense of the moment.

"If he got it right," wrote former SURFER editor Matt Warshaw in his fine biography *Photo: Stoner*, "the scene blinking through the lens would hit the film not just with color and shape, but also an emotional charge."

Stoner's status as SURFER's star image-maker also helped establish what was then a brand new protocol in which the period's hottest surfers, eager for exposure, would actually follow the photographer around, instead of the other way around—a practice still prevalent today.

By the late 1960s, Stoner's shadow was cast wide if not long (suffering from various mental illnesses, Stoner virtually stopped shooting in 1970, disappeared, and was eventually declared dead in 1991). Coming up in that shadow, however, were two young surfer/photographers named Art Brewer and Jeff Divine. To put their careers in perspective, simply compare them to Stoner's reign, which lasted all of four years. Brewer and Divine, whose photos began running in SURFER in '68 and '69 respectively, are still out there on the firing line, still getting the shot more than forty years later. During that tenure they've been joined on the masthead by many fine contemporaries. Steve Wilkings, Larry Pope, Warren Bolster, Bernie Baker, Woody Woodworth, Craig Peterson, Guy Motil, Craig Fineman,

Darrell Jones, Steve Sakamoto, Erik and Kirk Aeder, Tom Servais, Mike Moir, Peter Crawford, Dick Meseroll, Tom Dugan, Rob Gilley, and Ted Grambeau all make the short list of world-class photographers whose view through the aperture has shaped both our collective fantasy and reality; the surfing world has become as they have seen it. The latest generation of SURFER photographers has taken this precedent into the digital age, where, freed from messy film and creepy darkrooms, their eyes never close. Lensmen like Todd Glazer, Chris Burkhart, Anthony Ghiglia, and Brian Nevins are the guys hot surfers are following around these days.

And then there are photographers like Scott Aichner, backstroking out into pounding, 20-foot Puerto Escondido tubes, fiberglass camera housing cradled on his chest like a baby sea otter. Kicking hard against the current, lining up with quick glances over his shoulder, anticipating that singular moment when wave, surfer, and photographer find themselves aligned in a cosmic coincidence, capturing with the click of a shutter that which cannot truly be defined but only experienced. —SG

preceding spread: SHORE, SKY, CLOUDS, WAVE, SURFER; ALL THE COMPONENTS OF A CLASSIC WIDE-ANGLE PIPE SHOT PERFECTLY IN PLACE. MAKUA ROTHMAN.

above: AAMION GOODWIN, PIPELINE WRAPAROUND.

SURFER may have gone color back in 1962, but that hasn't meant black-and-white photography hasn't had a place in its pages. In fact, backlit conditions are still some of the trickiest to shoot in, and it's often just a case of pointing, pulling the trigger, and hoping for the best. In this instance, a late-afternoon bottom turn of Mark Healey's produced a surprisingly dramatic result.

MARK HEALEY, PIPELINE.

Churning rip currents, pounding impact zones, shifting lineups, speeding surfers with sharp board noses and fins—swimming out into the waves with a water housing and wide-angle lens is probably the most difficult form of surf photography. And when the surf spot is Pipeline, it's even harder than it looks. Mikala Jones slips into frame. ▬

Gone are the days when John Severson would find himself down on the beach at Pipeline, shooting alone with his Century 1000 mm. At the same moment this photo was taken there were probably fifty international photographers clustered on the sand, aiming their telephoto lens at this Pipeline peak. For longtime SURFER staffer Tom Servais, however, a low outcropping of rocks a quarter mile to the west provided the perfect perch on which to focus his 800 mm and capture one of the rarest images in the sport: a fresh Pipeline perspective of Bruce Irons. ▬

Shooting blue-water reef breaks like Sunset Beach is never a simple proposition—distant peaks, sea spray, and foreground waves are the photographer's nemesis. Former SURFER photo editor and legendary lensman Art Brewer has spent decades chronicling the North Shore and has the conditions wired enough to know when to pull out the big 1200 mm—and from what angle to use it. Michael "Munga" Barry, Sunset Beach, 1976. ▬

IF THE MAGAZINE HAD BEEN CALLED *SURF ACTION* OR SOME OTHER EASILY MARKETED BUT SELF-LIMITING TITLE, READERS WOULD'VE NEVER ENJOYED LIFESTYLE-
DEFINING VARIETY LIKE THIS: ❶ ULU WATU REVERIE. ❷ GOLDEN SILHOUETTE. ❸ UNNECESSARY CAUTION. ❹ TRESTLES EVENING AVIARY.

For the past decade, SURFER senior staff photographer Scott Aichner's wide-angle work has provided the magazine's readers with interior perspectives they'd otherwise never see. Case in point is Dean Brady's Puerto Escondido barrel: perfectly lit, perfectly composed, perfectly amazing. ═══

PHOTO DEPARTMENT

BY JEFF DIVINE

JEFF DIVINE

Line one, blinking: "Hi, Photo Department, this is Jeff." "Hey, Jeff. Love the new issue, really, seriously, one of the best ones you guys have ever done."

Line two: "Hey, I can't believe you guys got the wrong name on my shot, with all that I do for you. Do you realize how hard it is to swim out for four hours at Pipe and how little you pay? Do you know when the check is coming for my overweight baggage, car rental, and accommodations? What receipts? You can't ask for a receipt from an Indonesian baggage handler. You're lucky to get out of there alive, let alone get a receipt. Are you kidding? Also, in the future, please don't use any other photographers' work with mine. How many shots did I get in the photo feature?" "No, no, really we love your work, I've got five people in my office right now, can I call you back later?"

Line three: "Hi, this is Tommy's mom. Tommy is stuck in Bali on assignment for you and needs more money. . . . Oh, you didn't send him on assignment to Bali?"

Line four: "I just wanted to tell you a little bit about my son David; he's been beating all of the older kids in competitions, and I have some photos . . . "

Line five: "I'd like to order a print for my apartment."

Line six: "Sorry I didn't tell you earlier, we need three shots of the beach cleanup to ship to the printer in about an hour."

Line seven: "Your guests are waiting for you in the darkroom, the dart game is about to begin."

Line two: "There's an artist downstairs who'd like to show his work; he says he met you at Pipeline a long time ago."

Line three: "The advertiser is here with a trash bag full of transparencies—he's not sure which ones are SURFER's."

Line five: "Yes, hello. I resent the use of bikini-clad women in your magazine. My husband has had sex-addiction problems, and you have no idea how hard it is to protect him. And then, there it is staring him in the face in your new issue . . . "

Line six: "The advertiser is snapping; they think we airbrushed a logo off the cover shot, please come down to my office."

The photo desk at SURFER is a constant swirl of activity. The packages with photo disks arrive every day, while the ftp picture-drop site gets loaded twenty-four hours a day, and the e-mails with photos attached and phone calls come pouring in, aggressively describing the latest: The swell! The trip! The event! The portrait! The mood! The party! The surfboard! The firstborn's first wave! or Joey's first surf safari! When you add in the SURFER Web site, with its community forum, recent video clips, featured news, industry news, event calendar, WaveWatch forecasting, SURFER store, surf cams, fantasy surfer contest, and more, you can see that what we used to call "The Secret Thrill" is now common fodder.

Early on, the magazine spoke to an enamored audience of core surfers. They were unbranded, spoke their own language, and had their own heroes, territories, and antiestablishment way of looking at the world. A handful of photographers, mostly surfers themselves, tried to capture the moments the core audience understood and applauded, and sometimes succeeded. Each new location pictured in SURFER was studied closely, every aspect of the wave, where you parked, where you walked in, who was there, and when to go. Word of mouth was the soul of the sport. The low ASA film was difficult to expose and the 1000 mm lens almost impossible to follow focus. To know how the surf was, you went to the ocean and looked. A surf trip was an exciting, nervous step into the unknown. The photos in SURFER were like postcards you couldn't wait to receive.

By the late '80s, surfers were being paid when their photo appeared in the editorial spreads. The art and photo departments at SURFER went into a minor emotional free fall when the staff realized that some of the "Spicoliesque" surfers made more money from simply having a photo in the mag than they did in a year. As the garment world ramped up, another black day occurred when the photographers realized that a graphic designer made more for putting pin lines around a photo than a photographer got

for the photo itself that took hours of swimming in a dangerous setting to capture. This pay scale inequity remains. But the top photographers were simply in love with the craft, and most of them probably would have paid to do what they were doing.

By the late '80s the big surfwear companies were the dominant force in the star-making machine, and their various logos started to make the surfboard look more like a stock car. The world paid attention. Jackie O and Warhol had the latest issue of SURFER on their coffee tables. Lifestyle clothing brands were making millions, which drove magazine ad sales, and the magazine bulked up. The core surfer's dream fodder was still there—fantasy surf photos buried between the pages of ads. A famous Malibu surfer had a party, complete with valet parking, to celebrate his appearence on the cover of the magazine. That one cover photo would have sparked thousands of dollars in surfboard, wetsuit, and accessories sales. The foundation of the magazine was the surf photography, and the look was tack sharp (Fast Glass lenses) with front lighting (morning sun, called Larry light). Expensive explorations with accompanying writer, videographer, and highly ranked pro surfers became the norm. Surf photography became more competitive, with secret trips and instructions to "poach" photos of the surfers on the other trips. Heated arguments between the photographers on land and in the water became common. In 1970, there were a handful of active surf photographers. By 1981, there were 140 names in the files at SURFER. In 2009, there are more than six hundred.

The marketing of surfing lifestyle brands focused a lot more attention on the sport. A surfwear manufacturer's dream was still to have his surfer on the cover of SURFER, logo front and center, while also providing a good look at the product; a specific print design would sell out in the surf shops within days of being on a SURFER

cover. The garment lifestyle-brand world and the magazine creative side ran parallel, each unaware of how the other worked. The editorial staff at SURFER was shocked when an advertiser accused them of taking their logo off of a cover shot and poster insert (years before Photoshop). This kind of maneuver could mean thousands of dollars of lost income for the company. We had no idea what they were talking about and had to show the original photo to prove the point. In the photo department, we were so busy picking and getting the photos out to the printers and designers that the last thing we worried about was a logo. The truth came out some weeks later when a friend of a friend went to visit an artist who, with airbrush in hand and five large blowups of our competitor's cover shot, was working away to obscure a logo.

By the time Laird Hamilton got the cover shot (2000) with his epic barrel ride at Teahupoo, surfers were already considered the new American cowboy icon. Photos of Laird riding eight-story-tall waves at Jaws on Maui not only shocked real surfers but also brought the mainstream media with its public even closer to the water's edge. The pristine pineapple fields adjacent to the cliff overview at Jaws were trampled and overrun with hundreds of cars, tourists, videographers, and photographers, all drawn there by the SURFER photos. Laird was next featured zigzagging down a giant mountain of a wave for American Express. Laird became one of the most recognizable surfers of all time. Jack Johnson strummed his way to superstar musician, but deep down you know he still pines to be on the cover of SURFER. Real surfers don't care about all of the modern-day surf brouhaha. The perfectly shaped, perfectly empty surf-fantasy photo is what it's all about, even if you have to look through the entire magazine to get to it. And so long as surfers keep looking, the SURFER photo editor's phone will keep ringing.

DIVINE'S TOOLBOX.

RISKY BUSINESS

Although waves and boats are traditionally a bad combination, SURFER photographers have regularly risked capsizing in the surf to get close up to offshore action. Shooting from a boat with a 300 mm lens and a 1.4 converter, you provide that action. But one errant water splash from a surfer exiting the boat, a heavy gust of wind, or just an unexpected lurch of the boat can spell disaster. ▬

below: TEAHUPOO TERROR RIDE.
opposite: PERILOUS SURF ZONE PERSPECTIVE OF JORDY SMITH, INDONESIA.

THE NIKONOS

During the 1960s Ron Stoner became the master of the Nikonos, a compact, waterproof camera that was popular with skindivers at the time. Unlike cameras with more bulky water housings, the Nikonos was a snap to swim and position yourself with. The ease ended there: To get a sharp image you had to preset the focus and hope the your fast-moving subject would come into frame at just the right moment. All of which made Stoner's artistry with the Nikonos even more remarkable. Bill Fury at Huntington Pier, photo: Ron Stoner.

FLASH FILL

Today's custom-made water housings incorporate powerful Speed Lite flash units to give those sunrise shots an added boost. But artificial lighting or not, the photographer still has to set the alarm for 4:00 A.M., struggle into the hooded 4 mm wetsuit, swim out into the cold ocean, connect with the wave and surfer—and all with about a thirty-second window of opportunity. Ventura photographer David Puu won the Photo of the Year Award at the 2001 Surfer Poll for this foreground balanced shot of Dan Malloy in which all the abovementioned elements came together. ▬

THE 1,000 MM

Early in his career, SURFER founder John Severson bought this big bazooka of a lens from Century Lenses in Hollywood. While ordinarily used for wildlife photography, when applied to surfing it made shooting stills from shore a viable alternative. Although not exactly user-friendly—it was heavy and hard to focus and had a sketchy viewfinder—this very lens shared by SURFER senior photographers like Ron Stoner, Art Brewer, Steve Wilkings, Jeff Divine, Warren Bolster, and Craig Fineman took some of the greatest photos in SURFER history. ▬

① PAUL STRAUCH, HALEIWA, 1962. ② BARRY KANAIAUPUNI, SUNSET BEACH. ③ JOHN SEVERSON WITH THE SPORT'S MOST CELEBRATED LENS. ④ BILL HAMILTON, PUPUKEA.

FLASH WITH SLAVE UNIT

The competition in surf photography motivates the
search for unusual techniques. The photographer
can team up with a land-based shooter, swim out
with a flash slave unit, and coordinate the lighting,
making for dramatic, studio-setlike, stylized colors.
Kolohe Andino, Nicaragua. ▬

HANDHELD

SURFER photography has always leaned toward the involved. A water-shot appeared on its very third cover, in-the-tube photography in 1967, board-mounted cameras in 1976, and helicopter angles in 1984. Lately a growing number of surfers have discovered the thrill of recording their own moments of extreme surfing in the tube. Surfers like Brian Conley, Ken Collins, and Todd Morcom use a variety of techniques and equipment to bring back intimate portraits of their most intense moments. ▭

CAMERA BOARD

As far back as the 1950s, surf photography pioneer Dr. Don James was mounting cameras on the noses of his surfboard. But in 1974 SURFER staffer Steve Wilkings refined the design, attached it to the tail, and added a radio-control shutter release. Though unwieldy, under the feet of test pilots like Gerry Lopez and Rory Russell the results were spectacular. ▬

❶ THE MALIBU RACETRACK, AS SEEN FROM THE HANDHELD NIKONOS CAMERA OF RON STONER IN 1966. ❷ TODD MORCOM ADJUSTS THE SEVEN-POUND HOUSING WHILE SETTING UP TO PULL INTO THE WAVE AS IT PITCHES OUT, MAINLAND MEXICO. ❸ KEN "SKINDOG" COLLINS IS KNOWN AS AN "EXTREME" SURFER, AND IT TAKES JUST THAT SORT OF COMMITMENT TO TAKE A CAMERA ALONG FOR THE RIDE. ❹ THE LATE WARREN BOLSTER, A FORMER *SURFER* PHOTO EDITOR, TOOK THE CAMERA BOARD INTO THE NEW MILLENNIUM. **TAMAYO PERRY,** TEAHUPOO.

HELI SHOTS

At more than $700 per hour, helicopter surf photography is generally reserved for only the most epic days. Even so, it presents its own unique set of challenges—focusing on surf action while on a theme-park ride and not dropping your camera from six stories up, not the least of them. SURFER photogs like Sylvain Casenave, Tom Servais, and Sean Davey all have it wired. ▬

1 BUZZY KERBOX, PEAHI. **2** ZACH WORMHOUDT, MAVERICKS. **3** SHANE DORIAN, TEAHUPOO.

First utilized for tow-in surfing, the personal watercraft quickly became another vital tool for the surf photographer. In the mid-1990s, SURFER's groundbreaking stories on both Peahi on Maui and Mavericks in Northern California first hinted at the advantage of shooting off the ski: watershot action from an up-off-the-water perspective. Today the ski is instrumental in not only the discovery of dozens of new surf breaks—including a number of fearsome "slab" waves—but their documentation as well. ▬

THE MOMENT

following spread: Few issues of SURFER have been printed that don't include at least one photo of an empty wave: Freezing the ephemeral moment of a breaking wave can turn action photography into art. Just ask SURFER staff photographer Clark Little—brother of big-wave legend Brock Little—who appeared on *Good Morning America* to explain the technique involved in getting these incredible art-quality water shots. Clark made it sound simple: Take a digital camera, crouch down in some of the gnarliest shore-break on Earth, and prepare to get pounded silly. Beautiful. ▬

PHOTOGRAPHY AND ILLUSTRATION CREDITS

FRONT COVER: PHOTOGRAPH OF MARK HEALEY BY SCOTT AICHNER

BACK COVER: PHOTOGRAPH OF MIKE HYNSON BY RON STONER

PAGES 2-3: SAM OLSEN/TODD GLASER

PAGE 4: JOLI

PAGE 6: PETER CRAWFORD

PAGES 12-13: GRANT ELLIS

PAGE 15: JIM PERRY

PAGE 17: JOE CURREN

PAGE 18: (1) JASON KENWORTHY, (2) JOHN SEVERSON, (3) JEFF DIVINE

PAGE 19: (4) BRAD BARETT, (5) RON PERROT, (6) JEFF DIVINE

PAGE 21: SCOTT AICHNER

PAGE 22: RON STONER

PAGE 23: DON JAMES

PAGE 26: PETER FRENCH

PAGE 27: (2) JASON CHILDS, (3) JASON MURRAY

PAGE 28: (1) YASHA HETZEL, (2) TOM SERVAIS

PAGE 29: (4) (5) JASON CHILDS

PAGES 30-31: JASON CHILDS

PAGE 32: WARREN BOLSTER

PAGES 33, 35: CRAIG PETERSON

PAGE 36: (TOP) JEFF DIVINE, (BOTTOM) ERIK AEDER

PAGE 37: (TOP) JEFF DIVINE, (MIDDLE) ROB KEITH, (BOTTOM) JEFF DIVINE

PAGE 39: TOM SERVAIS

PAGES 42-43: TED GRAMBEAU

PAGES 44-45: SURFER ARCHIVE

PAGE 47: (BOTTOM) MARK GORDON

PAGE 48: (1) MACGILLIVRAY/FREEMAN, (2) PETER CRAWFORD, (3) (4) TOM SERVAIS, (5) ART BREWER

PAGE 49: (6) JEFF DIVINE, (7) BERNIE BAKER, (8) RON STONER

PAGE 51: TOM SERVAIS

PAGE 52: JEREMIAH KLEIN

PAGE 53: TODD GLASER

PAGES 55-57: ART BREWER

PAGES 58-59: MATT GEORGE

PAGE 60: ART BREWER

PAGE 61: (TOP) RON STONER, (BOTTOM) SURFER ARCHIVE

PAGE 62: TOM SERVAIS

PAGES 66-67: GRANT ELLIS

PAGE 68: PETER GOWLAND

PAGES 70-71: BERNIE BAKER

PAGES 72-73, 75: SCOTT AICHNER

PAGE 76: (1) CAMPBELL COLLECTION, (2) WARREN BOLSTER, (3) TOM SERVAIS

PAGE 77: (4) JASON KENWORTHY, (5) RON STONER, (6) SURFER ARCHIVE, (7) JEFF DIVINE, (8) SURFER ARCHIVE, (9) RON STONER

PAGE 78: (1) JEFF DIVINE, (2) SURFER ARCHIVE, (3) TOM SERVAIS

PAGE 79: (4) RON STONER, (5) GUY MOTIL, (6) JEFF DIVINE

PAGE 81: PETER CRAWFORD

PAGES 82-83, 85: JEFF DIVINE

PAGE 87: (TOP) JASON KENWORTHY, (BOTTOM) ERIK AEDER

PAGES 88-89: JEFF DIVINE

PAGE 90: SURFER ARCHIVE

PAGE 91: (3) JASON MURRAY, (4) JEFF DIVINE

PAGES 92-93: JASON KENWORTHY

PAGE 95: JASON KENWORTHY

PAGE 96: (1) SURFER ARCHIVE, (2) RON STONER

PAGE 97: (3) JEFF DIVINE, (4) (5) SURFER ARCHIVE

PAGES 100-101: JEFF DIVINE

PAGES 102-103: TOM SERVAIS

PAGE 105: JASON MURRAY

PAGE 106: (1) JOHN SEVERSON, (2) SCOTT AICHNER

PAGE 107: (3) BERNIE BAKER, (4) ART BREWER, (5) (6) TOM SERVAIS

PAGE 108: JASON CHILDS

PAGE 109: (2) TOM SERVAIS, (3) (4) JASON CHILDS, (5) RON STONER

PAGE 111: JASON CHILDS

PAGE 113: REBECCA NORDQUIST

PAGE 115: TOM SERVAIS

PAGE 118: JEFF DIVINE

PAGE 119: (2) TIM MCKENNA, (3) SHORTY

PAGE 120: TOM SERVAIS

PAGE 121: JILL BLUNK

PAGE 123: (1) KAREN/ASP, (2) TOM SERVAIS, (3) JEFF DIVINE, (4) RON STONER, (5) BILL MORRIS (6) TOM SERVAIS, (7) (8) JEFF DIVINE, (9) CRAIG FINEMAN, (10) JASON CHILDS

PAGE 124: MARCUS COLLECTION

PAGE 126: TODD GLASER

PAGES 128-129: JASON KENWORTHY

PAGES 130-131: MIKE MOIR

PAGE 132: SURFER ARCHIVE

PAGE 134: (1) ART BREWER, (2) KEN SEINO

PAGE 135: (4) RON STONER, (5) SURFER ARCHIVE, (6) GRANT ELLIS, (7) SURFER ARCHIVE, (8) STEVE SAKAMOTO, (9) KEN SEINO

PAGE 136: (1) (2) GRANT ELLIS

PAGE 137: (3) GRANT ELLIS, (4) JASON CHILDS, (5) TODD GLASER.

PAGES 138-139: TOM SERVAIS

PAGES 141-143: JEFF DIVINE

PAGE 144: RON STONER

PAGE 146: TOM SERVAIS

PAGE 147: BERNIE BAKER

PAGE 148: BILL CLEARY

PAGE 149: SURFER ARCHIVE

PAGES 150-151: JASON CHILDS

PAGES 152, 154-155: JEFF DIVINE

PAGE 156: (2) JEFF DIVINE

PAGE 157: (3) (5) JEFF DIVINE

PAGE 158: WITZIG COLLECTION

PAGES 160-161: PHIL ROBERTS

PAGES 162-165: SCOTT AICHNER

PAGE 166-167: JEFF DIVINE

PAGE 168: SCOTT AICHNER

PAGE 169: (TOP) TOM SERVAIS, (BOTTOM) ART BREWER

PAGE 170: (1) ANTHONY GHIGLIA, (2) SCOTT AICHNER

PAGE 171: (3) GRANT ELLIS, (4) TOM SERVAIS

PAGES 172-173: SCOTT AICHNER

PAGE 174: SONNY MILLER

PAGE 175: SURFER ARCHIVE

PAGE 176: (TOP) JASON KENWORTHY, (BOTTOM) SEAN DAVEY

PAGE 177: RON STONER

PAGES 178-179: DAVID PUU

PAGE 180: (1) JOHN SEVERSON, (2) JEFF DIVINE

PAGE 181: (3) SURFER ARCHIVE, (4) ART BREWER

PAGES 182-183: GRANT ELLIS/TODD GLASER

PAGE 184: (1) RON STONER, (2) ANTHONY GHIGLIA

PAGE 185: (3) KEN "SKINDOG" COLLINS, (4) WARREN BOLSTER

PAGE 186: TOM SERVAIS

PAGE 187: (2) FRANK QUIARTE, (3) JOLI

PAGES 188-189: CLARK LITTLE

FOR HELPING PROVE THAT THE RIDE CAN LAST FOREVER I'D LIKE TO THANK DR. RAYMOND E. GEORGE, CAPT. U.S.N. (RET); JIMMY HUNTER, SENSEI AND SPIRITUAL SURF GUIDE; AND MOST IMPORTANTLY VIRENIA PEEPLES, WHO WILL ALWAYS BE MY "KIANI."
— SG

LIBRARY OF CONGRESS CATALOGING-IN-PUBLICATION DATA AVAILABLE

ISBN: 978-0-8118-7034-4

MANUFACTURED IN CHINA

DESIGN BY ANNE DONNARD

10 9 8 7 6 5 4 3 2 1

CHRONICLE BOOKS
680 SECOND STREET
SAN FRANCISCO, CALIFORNIA 94107

WWW.CHRONICLEBOOKS.COM